ten poems to open your heart

also by roger housden

Chasing Rumi:
A Fable About Finding the
Heart's True Desire

Ten Poems to Change Your Life

Sacred America:
The Emerging Spirit of the People

ten poems

to

open

your

heart

ROGER HOUSDEN

HARMONY BOOKS
NEW YORK

Published by Harmony Books, New York, New York.
Member of the Crown Publishing Group,
a division of Random House, Inc.

www.randomhouse.com

Harmony Books is a registered trademark and
the Harmony Books colophon is a trademark
of Random House, Inc.

*A complete list of credits for previously
published material appears at the end of the book.*

Printed in the United States of America

Design by Karen Minster

Library of Congress Cataloging-in-Publication Data
Housden, Roger.
    Ten poems to open your heart / Roger Housden.
    Includes bibliographical references.
    1. Love poetry, English.   2. Love poetry—
Translations into English.   3. Love poetry—History
and criticism.   I. Title.

PN6110.L6 T43 2003
811'.6—dc21   2002017256
                    ISBN 1-4000-4563-0

10   9   8   7   6   5   4   3   2   1

FIRST EDITION

Contents

Introduction

Hafiz,
Awake awhile.
Just one True moment of Love
Will last for days.[1]

What is it that flies free when the heart springs open? Love tumbles out in all of its colors. Tears flow for the sadness of the world; joy pours forth in the embrace of a lover; a tiny wren becomes precious to our eyes; people in the street carry the same cross, the same beauty, as we do. Life, God, call it what you will, is alive and well again, and all things shall be well, whatever they are.

When the heart opens, we forget ourselves and the world pours in: this world, and also the invisible world of meaning that sustains everything that was and ever shall be. When the heart opens, everything matters, and this world and the next become one and the same.

Great poetry, like great art, is a bridge between our heart and the heart of the world. Mary Oliver has said many beautiful

things. In her book *The Leaf and the Cloud,* she speaks of a poem
this way:

> *It wants to open itself,*
> *like the door of a little temple,*
> *so that you might step inside and be cooled and refreshed,*
> *and less yourself than part of everything.*[2]

That is what happens when the heart door opens—you
become "less yourself than part of everything." Many are the
sentinels who guard that door: our fears, our self-importance,
our meanness, our greed, our bitterness, and others. Yet one
good poem can slip past them all.

I believe that any one of the ten poems in this book can
open that door and let your love fly free. That, in any event,
is what they have done for me. I look into their mirrors and
see my own heart reflected there.

While the subject of love is the essence of every one of
these poems, they are not all love poems in the conventional
sense. The term is commonly used to describe poetry whose
subject is passionate love, often sexual, nearly always romantic. While some of the ten poems are certainly romantic, and
the setting for another is the marriage bed, the love that is
set free here includes, but is not restricted to, that between a
man and a woman.

Love, like everything else, exists in a spectrum. Love of
another, love of the world, love of God, all these loves are
really one love in different degrees of light and density. That
is why lovers of God so often use sexual imagery to describe

their experience of the ineffable. The heat of sexual and emotional love cools into a subtler, but no less passionate fire as it rises to the heart, where it fans out to include others and the world. It cools still further as it merges into the wordless sphere of the invisible.

Yet the hottest flame—white heat—is the coolest to the touch. There are few poets, after all, more passionate than those lovers of God, Rumi, Hafiz, and Saint John of the Cross. In the quote above, Mary Oliver makes it clear how the temple of her poem, too, is meant to be cooling.

Love would be explainable if it were only a matter of a linear arrangement of intensities and colors. It isn't, of course. In the red flame there may be touches of blue and yellow; in the white, perhaps a shade of orange. In the deepest abandon of sexual love, wings can sprout from your shoulders. In the same way, the love for which the only language is silence can be tinged with an ecstasy that makes your whole body shudder.

You will find many of the colors of love in this book, and your own experience will probably give different tones to each of them. You will also find a hint of the colorless love that is beyond even the metaphor of a band of light: the love that sustains everything that can ever be, the dark as well as the light of the world.

I cannot claim to be anything more than a fool when it comes to love. Its winds have ripped the clothes from my back more than once. At times, it is true, I have found safe harbor in its port, though even there my anchor has slipped sometimes, not being fastened in solid enough ground. In my experience, personal love has always carried the signature of something beyond itself, deeper than—though including—physical attraction and the sharing of interests. I can only imagine that must always be so, for how can an ego love anything other than its own needs and desires?

When we love one another deeply, we engage the soul; and the soul, whose nature is relatedness, feels all things. The soul also knows, or at least suspects, that its love, in fact, comes from beyond itself, from a source we can never know. That's why love can so easily make fools of us. It is like the air: impossible to grasp yet everywhere, impossible to fix into a social or moral code, never subject to strategy or calculation, always and ever free of our preconceptions.

That is why love is so dangerous. It is always unpremeditated. You can never know when it will strike you, how to live in its intensity once it has, or when it will leave, if indeed a love that is true can ever leave. That is why this book is not a series of lessons on love—poetry, in any event, was never the best medium for preaching.

No, what you have here is the sudden revelation, a shout of wonder, the jaw dropped open. Get ready, the poet says. At any moment—in this moment—love can burst into your world and perhaps change it forever. Be warned, though: once your heart has blown open and love has found its way into your bloodstream, the time may come when it requires of you a great work that will not cease until you have become ashes.

These love revelations are captured in the medium of poetry. Great poetry happens when the mind is looking the other way and words fall from the sky to shape a moment that would normally be untranslatable. Great poems are

icons. They capture the moment of vision and offer a door-
way into realms unavailable to our daylight eyes and to our
rational capacities.

Yet the strange thing is, when you enter a poem with your
heart as well as your mind, a tremor of recognition will run
through you. You *know* what the poet is saying, but you know
it viscerally, not with your body of information. This is never
so true as with a poem whose subject is love. Because we
know what love is despite ourselves. We long for it, pray for it;
we mourn its parting; yet that longing, as Rumi tells us, "IS
the secret cup."[3] We are perhaps never so close than when
we most poignantly feel its absence. Then, we may wonder
whether love, after all, ever goes anywhere. Perhaps it is we
who walk away.

The ten poems begin with a clarion call from Mary Oliver, a
call to follow our love whatever the consequences. Sharon
Olds leads us toward the holy ground that can emerge out of
making love. Galway Kinnell reminds us that everything "flowers, from within, of self-blessing"; Naomi Shihab Nye gives
extraordinary insight into the meaning of kindness; Pablo
Neruda's love for his wife transcends death. Robert Bly names
the third presence that can exist between a man and a woman.
And Rumi leads us to the love that burns us to smoke.

If there is one theme that runs through these poems
more than any other, it is that the open heart of love is to be
found in embracing our frailties, our mortality, the clay of
our human nature. The book follows the downward, rather
than the upward spiritual path. It is by traveling down into
their darkness—by allowing the full experience of their

humanness—that most of these poets find their way to a clearer, brighter light. Even Rumi, a Sufi mystic and saint, found his deepest ecstasy by falling headlong into the waters of grief, which washed over him when his beloved teacher, Shams, was killed.

In the first book in this series, *Ten Poems to Change Your Life*, I said that all the poems could be condensed into one single command—Wake up and Love! (But that "something great would be lost then . . . the enchantment of the telling.") This is truer than ever in this present work, whose entire subject is love itself. For what is it that breaks the heart open, if not love in any of its guises? (For those who wish, on reading this book, to read more of these poets, the work of four of them—Mary Oliver, Pablo Neruda, Galway Kinnell, and Rumi—is also represented in *Ten Poems to Change Your Life*.)

Many readers of the first book have written to tell me that the format—a poem followed by a personal exploration of the theme, rather than by academic criticism—allowed them to appreciate poetry in a way they had never done before. It also encouraged them to use the poems as windows onto the deep questions and concerns at the hearts of their own lives.

That book, like this new one, was first and foremost about those deep questions and feelings. The poems, and my reflections on them, were the vehicle. I am not, then, a professor—a professional in the realm of poetry or literature. In her Nobel Lecture, Wislawa Szymborska says that in reality there are no professors of poetry. "This would mean, after all, that poetry is an occupation requiring specialized study, regular examinations, theoretical articles with bibliographies attached . . . and this would mean, in turn, that it's not enough to cover pages with even the most exquisite poems in order to become a poet."

I am glad to be an amateur—a word whose roots lie in the Italian *amatore,* a "lover." I am a wonderer, an explorer of life's deeper currents, and my exploration has, in the last few years, turned to poetry. Perhaps it is by virtue of my amateur status (a venerable English, if not American tradition) that the poems that most easily capture my attention are those with an accessible style and language. In both books, I needed the poems to be direct and immediate, and many readers who have normally felt intimidated by poetry have told me that the choice of poems dissolved their anxiety in this regard.

Yet my first criterion for choosing these ten poems to open your heart was whether or not they did just what the title said they could do. My own heart is closed as often as it is open, which is why I am thankful for poems like these, able as they are to breach my defenses. That, more than any managed concern about having an even spread of poets from different countries, or times, or a balanced representation of male and female poets, determined the final choice. (In the event, the balance turned out pretty equal.)

The same format, then, is followed in both books. I cannot emphasize enough that my reflections rely less on book learning than on my own life experience. They are invitations to plumb for yourself the depths of the meanings you find in the poems, perhaps by way of contrast to my own associations. *Ten Poems to Open Your Heart* is not a work of literary criticism, but it will be, I hope, a source of inspiration.

Finally, the poems are a tribute to the resonance that lives in you, the reader, who has picked up this book. You, who know love when you feel it—who know, along with Rumi, that

> *All the particles in the world*
> *Are in love and looking for lovers.*
> *Pieces of straw tremble*
> *In the presence of amber.*[4]

1

WEST WIND #2

by Mary Oliver

*You are young. So you know everything. You leap
into the boat and begin rowing. But listen to me.
Without fanfare, without embarrassment, without
any doubt, I talk directly to your soul. Listen to me.
Lift the oars from the water, let your arms rest, and
your heart, and heart's little intelligence, and listen to
me. There is life without love. It is not worth a bent
penny, or a scuffed shoe. It is not worth the body of a
dead dog nine days unburied. When you hear, a mile
away and still out of sight, the churn of the water
as it begins to swirl and roil, fretting around the
sharp rocks—when you hear that unmistakable
pounding—when you feel the mist on your mouth
and sense ahead the embattlement, the long falls
plunging and steaming—then row, row for your life
toward it.*

Row for Your Life

"Poetry is a life-cherishing force. For poems are not words, after all, but fires for the cold, ropes let down to the lost, something as necessary as bread in the pockets of the hungry. Yes indeed."
>   MARY OLIVER,
>   *A Poetry Handbook*[1]

Yes indeed! I can still feel the heat of Mary Oliver's poem long after I have put it down. It is a prose poem, and one of the most deeply passionate poems on love that I have ever read. Mary Oliver is speaking directly to the way we live. The love in question is of the kind that feeds the whole garden of a life. What does it feel like to live a life of love? What does it take; and what is the alternative? These are the questions that burn through this poem.

Oliver, one of the most lyrical poets alive today, speaks plainly here; she has chosen to convey her message in prose. Her choice fits the poem's plain and declarative style. When I read this poem, however, I feel it is not so much she who makes these declarations, as that part of me who recognizes the truth of them. To read this poem aloud is to have the wiser part of yourself counsel the younger, untested heart that lives in us all.

> *You are young. So you know everything. You leap*
> *into the boat and begin rowing.*

Even now, at the age of fifty-seven, and for all the experience that has tried to teach me otherwise, there is a part of me, still young, that is tempted to leap into the boat and start rowing. I can still act as if I know everything. I can pile into an idea or a course of action before I have barely given it the time of day, with what can seem like an arrogant certainty. This is what Oliver calls "the heart's little intelligence": the impulsive response of a heart governed by the emotion of the moment.

In that moment, however, full of the rush of my own sense of capability, I feel as if I am getting on with the task at hand. Action is needed, and I'm taking it. Perhaps it's in my hard wiring: most men feel good when they fix things. Sometimes too late, it dawns on me how such "effectiveness" can rip at the fabric of things and discount the filaments of connection that join any one life to another.

> *But listen to me.*
> *Without fanfare, without embarrassment, without*
> *any doubt, I talk directly to your soul.*

"Listen to me": Oliver calls out three times. It is always three times that the cock crows. She calls, not to the youth in us, not to the impulsive heart that knows and sees the world with a naïve and definite clarity; she speaks to our soul. The soul knows in a different way. It gathers honey in the dark from near and far. The soul is always connected to a larger life. It is joined by invisible threads to the soul of all other things, and in this way, the world whispers to it without ceasing. That is why it is natural for the soul to pause, to listen, to wonder. Only the soul in us has the time to listen deeply.

If this poem is full of words consonant with sound—"the churn of the water . . . that unmistakable pounding . . . the long falls plunging and steaming"—it is because of this: that Oliver is addressing that part of us which is willing to listen in the dark, and willing to know with a knowing that is more of a shiver than a string of bright words.

There is life without love.

Mary Oliver is speaking directly to that part of you and me that knows, however faintly, that when we rush into life, when we leap into action without any connection to the deeper currents that move through us always, we are acting without love. Our oars thrash at the water, and we break the gossamer web of life this way.

There is indeed a life without love, she says. It is quite possible to live a life in which your soul plays no part. You can jump up and down with every passing impulse, and never hear the whispering call that is there all along. On the other hand, you can live a busy, efficient existence full of duties and responsibilities and never even know there is a deeper life. You can be successful, a bright star, even. But your nights may carry other voices on the wings of dreams. Whispers of great empty spaces, lonely and afraid.

Life without love—without the soul being wholly engaged in your living—is not worth a bent penny. Not just a penny, but a bent penny. Not just a single shoe, which is worthless without its partner, but a scuffed shoe. The bent penny and the scuffed shoe are degraded, somehow; their original form has been bent out of shape. Then, not just a dead dog, but a dead dog nine days unburied. Life without love stinks. These are some of the most shocking, awakening images I know of. Oliver is entirely uncompromising here; fierce, even. She does not fudge. If you will give no room for the soul in your life, then you might as well give up on the game now.

This is why she is calling so urgently here, not to the untested heart that jumps with every passing emotion, but to the truth of your deep heart. Every spiritual tradition makes a distinction between the two. The Christians call the latter the interior heart; the Hindus, the heart within the heart. The soul is its other name.

Mary Oliver is calling to your soul. It is a call you will find echoing through all her work. Mary Oliver, Pulitzer prize—winner, winner of the National Book Award, is one of the few great voices in American literature today who urges us to love this world with astonishment and devotion. "You do not have to be good," she declares (in her poem "Wild Geese"[2]); to Be, and to be awake—that, her poetry sings out, is the holiest thing.

Your soul, she suggests, is already connected to the bigger life that joins you to everything else. Let us call that bigger life by its true name, which is love. Mary Oliver is speaking not only of the love for another here, though that may be one way your own soul travels, as mine has. She is speaking more broadly about your life as a whole: whether its overall movement is one of love, or one of alienation.

When you hear that call, she says, when you feel in your marrow the pull of your soul—to another human being, to a work, to the true direction of your life—that is the time to act. Without that inner prompting, which you can hear only when you lay down your oars and listen in the quiet; without that, you will be like a boat without a rudder in life, however much control you may appear to have. Even though the source of the magnetic pull is still out of sight, even though you can't possibly know where it will lead you, though it may seem to be beyond all reason—to be madness, even—you must respond to it.

Trust and courage are qualities of soul, and you will need them both to follow the path of love. Which doesn't mean you won't feel trepidation, dread, even. But your fear and anxiety will be held in the broad embrace of a deeper trust whose source is love itself, the soul's air.

> *the churn of the water*
> *as it begins to swirl and roil, fretting around the*
> *sharp rocks—*

I first experienced the wildness of love when I was thirty years old. It was no easy ride, and my heart was pounding. Never before then had I fallen in love so completely, without reserve. It happened all of a sudden, with someone I had known well for years. One evening we were sitting with others in a room in London, as we had done so many times before. Our gaze met, and in that moment, a bolt of lightning passed between us. The intensity was so great, so unexpected, that I had to look away. The shock was too much to bear. From that moment on, we both felt as if the other was intimately present with us, day and night, wherever we were. From then on, whenever our eyes met, our bodies and minds were filled with the presence of an intense aliveness.

This woman, however, was the wife of one of my best friends and colleagues. I, too, was married, and my wife was pregnant. An old, old story, in which there is no lack of swirling and roiling. But was it love, or was it infatuation? Was it the call of the soul or the impulse of the untried heart, which had never known such wild intensity before? It is not always easy to know the difference, especially when the certainty of the young, impulsive part of us can be so convincing.

Webster's dictionary says *infatuation* is "to be inspired with a foolish or extravagant love." That certainly fits the description, though who is to say after the event if any love is foolish? The longing we had to be in each other's presence could not possibly be denied; yet to act on it decisively would have caused deep suffering for both our partners and our children. In the event, our lives led us away from each other within a few months, and what seemed at the time like the more difficult road, the call of duty—though now I sense it to have been the wisdom of some deeper stream—won out.

Our partners still suffered, of course, and as it happened, years later, both marriages ended.

After those few brief months, I did not see or hear of the woman whose eyes I had seen across that room for another twenty years. When we did finally meet again, on another continent, we still carried the memory of those fiery times, and realized that we continued to see each other in its reflection. Yet the intensity had died down long before, and our lives had moved on. There was no going back, and there were no regrets. Only a certain astonishment at how a love never dies, even so; and at the way life had picked us up, whirled us around, and set us down again on a path quite different from the one we had briefly imagined might be our destiny.

You will interpret Mary Oliver's words according to your own life circumstance. Only you, in a quiet moment of receptivity, can know the difference between your soul's true direction and the convincing clamor of your life's current intensity. Wherever you are in your life, her lines call out to you to let yourself fall headlong into the life that has been waiting for you all along. And whatever the circumstance, if it is a matter of love, it will be the ride of your life.

Not only that: it may well be the death of you—of the you that has refused to listen for so long, who has dared live only in a corner of your life, rather than reach out and bite the full fruit of it. When you hear the sound of that deep current, Mary Oliver says—"that unmistakable pounding"—then *row!* Think about it—she is urging us to head for the almighty drop, sight unseen, "a mile / away and still out of sight, . . . "

"[R]ow for your life / toward it." When you row, you have your back facing the direction you are heading toward. Even in this final moment, in this last line, Mary Oliver is saying it again: you cannot hope to see what lies ahead when it comes to a life lived with love. You can only row, drawn on by the soundless sound, knowing there is nothing else you can do or would even want to do.

What an astounding call. To strike out into the current that was there all along, rather than try so hard to push this way and that by your own efforts; to row along with it and sail over the waterfall into the bright air of love. Only much later in my life did I come to have that experience. Fully committed, not even having to know fully to what.

2

THE KNOWING

by Sharon Olds

Afterwards, when we have slept, paradise-
comaed, and woken, we lie a long time
looking at each other.
I do not know what he sees, but I see
eyes of surpassing tenderness
and calm, a calm like the dignity
of matter. I love the open ocean
Blue-grey-green of his iris, I love
the curve of it against the white,
that curve the sight of what has caused me
to come, when he's quite still, deep
inside me. I have never seen a curve
like that, except the earth from outer
space. I don't know where he got
his kindness without self-regard,
almost without self, and yet
he chose one woman, instead of the others.
By knowing him, I get to know

the purity of the animal
which mates for life. Sometimes he is slightly
smiling, but mostly he just gazes at me gazing,
his entire face lit. I love
to see it change if I cry—there is no worry,
no pity, a graver radiance. If we
are on our backs, side by side,
with our faces turned fully to face each other,
I can hear a tear from my lower eye
hit the sheet, as if it is an early day on earth,
and then the upper eye's tears
braid and sluice down through the lower eyebrow
like the invention of farming, irrigation, a non-nomadic people.
I am so lucky that I know him.
This is the only way to know him.
I am the only one who knows him.
When I wake again, he is still looking at me,
as if he is eternal. For an hour
we wake and doze, and slowly I know
that though we are sated, though we are hardly
touching, this is the coming the other
coming brought us to the edge of—we are entering,
deeper and deeper, gaze by gaze,
this place beyond the other places,
beyond the body itself, we are making
love.

Follow the Gaze

She is known for speaking the poetry of the body with eloquent directness; she has been praised for the accuracy and care with which she observes the body's physical acts, for how she paints in words the subtleties of our thinking and feeling. Sharon Olds does all this in this poem, and yet she does more. Here, her sensibility reaches below my thoughts, below the quiver in the muscle, to the flow of the presence that lovemaking can lead to.

It seemed to jar slightly, the phrase "paradise-comaed," when first I read it. Yet how else would you describe that deep kind of slumber that follows the fullness of making love? The Greek *koma* means a "deep sleep"; we use the word to indicate a profound unconsciousness. In those moments after we ease our bodies away from each other, we often do slip down several floors in the regions of consciousness. And if this coma is likened to paradise, perhaps it is because of the deep rest it spreads for a few moments, like a warm comforter, over body and mind.

The love Sharon Olds describes with such delicacy in this poem streams gently through the eyes, which are, after all, the windows of the soul. "The Knowing" is a poem of the gaze. The timeless time she is giving attention to is the afterglow; when she is looking at him looking at her, in between moments of paradise coma.

The first great singer-poets of love in the West, the troubadours of medieval Europe, spoke of love as "the seizure that comes from the meeting of the eyes." Joseph Campbell, the American mythologist, took up the troubadour's language and style when he said,

> So through the eyes love attains the heart, for the eyes are the scouts of the heart. . . . And when they are in full accord and firm, all three, in one resolve, at that time perfect love is born from what the eyes have made welcome to the heart. For as all true lovers know, love is perfect kindness, which is born, there is no doubt, from the heart and the eyes.[1]

What Sharon Olds receives from her lover's gaze is a "surpassing tenderness / and calm." What a gift that must be, for a woman to receive that from a man. The other way around might be more common. But a man usually has to fall deep into himself to bestow tenderness and calm; deep into the true strength and confidence of his masculinity, all too often buried beneath the anxieties of making a mark in the world and being a competent performer. When that masculine calm emerges, it is indeed the rock of ages, a solid substance, light as air, a mark of the true nobility of manhood.

Pause for a moment and consider this, the iris of your lover, and the curve of it against the white. This poem is personal to the writer, but only in a sense. She is the *I* in it, but then, so are we. Its greatness is in giving voice to the universal. We all remember, somewhere in the recesses of memory, if not in this moment, the eyes of a lover. But how rare it is to penetrate our feelings for those eyes, to even begin to make conscious what happens when our lover gazes at us; and especially in this precious time that Sharon Olds is attending to.

It's true, the eyes of my wife often send me falling over waterfalls. She has Botticelli eyes, large white pools and a yellow-green glint showering both a tenderness and an inducement to lie down in sweet pastures. But never have I thought to compare the curve of those eyes with the earth seen from outer space. The awe, the wonder of it; the sheer beauty of it. There's some deep reverence that the photo of earth taken from space arouses. That same reverence for life can awaken, Sharon Olds shows me, in beholding the planet of my lover's eye.

Joseph Campbell, in the quote above, says that "love is perfect kindness, which is born, there is no doubt, from the heart and the eyes." Olds knows this. She can feel the transmission of her lover's kindness through his eyes. And the nature of it is an absence of self-regard, which must surely be the essential condition of love. Love, then, is not the assuaging of some need, sexual, emotional, or otherwise. It is not greedy, clinging, wanting. It is the deep rest of the ocean floor. In that rest, kindness is passed on the breath.

Naomi Shihab Nye, in the poem of hers that is in this book, speaks of "the tender gravity of kindness." The kindness that Sharon Olds alludes to is not disturbed by tears; it simply becomes a "graver radiance." The kindness of love has substance, then. To be so at home in the company of tears, I suspect that this depth of kindness must have arisen from a knowledge of sorrow.

For a man, it can be disconcerting sometimes when the woman he has just made love with starts weeping. What old wounds has he uncovered? Are there things she is not telling him? But in the field of this kindness, such worries will not arise. The tears are more likely tears of relief, of happiness, of almost unbearable gratitude, even. Whatever their source, kindness knows that it is just what it is meant to be. Kindness has room.

The woman in Sharon Olds's poem is lying there between waking and sleeping, having just made love, marveling at the fact that her beloved chose one woman, instead of the others. He is without self-regard, "almost without self," yet enough of a "somebody" must have remained to have chosen her. A few lines later, she returns to the same sentiment, saying

I am the only one who knows him.

There is a purity, she says, in mating for life. Olds is clear: it is one man in particular she is speaking about. As universal as this poem is, it does not contain a word of abstraction. The universal is firmly rooted in the concrete experience of the love of one other human being. Talking about universal love is easy; to love one person is a humbling commitment.

Quite recently, Sharon Olds and her husband of many years parted. For years before then, she wrote dozens of poems in praise of their love, including this one. And now, what was once for a lifetime is over. Or is it? Does it detract from their love that their lives took an unthinkable turn? I do not think so. At the time of writing this poem, Sharon Olds's love was forever. Its beauty was forever. Nothing can change that. She knew that sense of eternity, and she passes it on to us, with courage, in full knowledge that nothing in this world is certain. We do not blame the rose when it drops its petals. She is now writing poems of grief, another kind of love. In her book-length poem *The Leaf and the Cloud*, Mary Oliver has this to say:

> *Do you think the grass is growing so wild and thick*
> *for its own life?*
> *Do you think the cutting is the ending, and not, also,*
> *a beginning?*
> *This is the world.*[2]

The two lovers in Sharon Olds's poem are truly in the garden of beauty that we lie in when we make love of a kind marked by the deepest tenderness. Is there anything more primordial, more resonant of Eden? However full our days are of toil and worry, the moments after lovemaking like this return us to our original beauty. "[H]e is still looking at me, / as if he is eternal." She can hear a tear falling, "hit the sheet, as if it is an early day on earth, . . . " We are washed by such intimacy with another. That innocence, which carries a memory somehow of those early days on earth, is there in all of us, always; but it is the gift of a lover to reveal us to ourselves in this way.

The way this poem ends is masterful. How does she do this? Put into form something we may know but so rarely have the words or even the understanding to say? The physical ecstasy of orgasm is itself a gateway to something beyond the body and beyond the mind. Sharon Olds's poetry plunges deeply into the personal detail of her own life, and yet with such intensity that she transports us through to an archetypal experience. She sanctifies ordinary life this way, shines a light around the edges of the body and joins it to spirit.

The road to this new country is the gaze. Traveling deeper and deeper down into each other's eyes—into each other's souls—"we are entering . . ."

> *this place beyond the other places,*
> *beyond the body itself, we are making*
> *love.*

Is this the deep knowledge implied by the poem's title? If so, those biblical authors may have known more than we gave them credit for. Most Bible readers assume the term (he "knew" her) to have been a polite euphemism for making love. In using a title with biblical overtones, Sharon Olds adds emphasis to the suggestion that, in making love, her lovers have entered onto holy ground.

When lovers fall beyond themselves—into that "coming the other / coming brought us to the edge of"—they enter the place which is the source of love. There, in some mysterious way, they participate in the making of the love that, itself, is continually making the world. This kind of love requires no touch of the skin, only an immersion in the presence that is always so. Through the door of this shining poem, Sharon Olds takes us right there.

3

SAINT FRANCIS AND THE SOW

by Galway Kinnell

The bud
stands for all things,
even for those things that don't flower,
for everything flowers, from within, of self-blessing;
though sometimes it is necessary
to reteach a thing its loveliness,
to put a hand on the brow
of the flower
and retell it in words and in touch
it is lovely
until it flowers again from within, of self-blessing;
as Saint Francis
put his hand on the creased forehead
of the sow, and told her in words and in touch
blessings of the earth on the sow, and the sow
began remembering all down her thick length,

from the earthen snout all the way
through the fodder and slops to the spiritual curl of the tail,
from the hard spininess spiked out from the spine
down through the great broken heart
to the blue milken dreaminess spurting and shuddering
from the fourteen teats into the fourteen mouths sucking
    and blowing beneath them:
the long, perfect loveliness of sow.

The Flower of Self-Blessing

This is one of those poems that acts on me cell by cell. It softens me, fills me with a reverence for the living world, and brings me into the fold of all living things. Even the sorrow of those times when I have felt apart, unworthy, without any hand to guide me to the deeper memory of my own belonging, even this weight is gathered up by the lines of this poem and brought into the light of a compassionate regard. It is a blessing poem, full of that ancient power that can revive even the brokenhearted.

If you let your mind and your tongue savor these first two lines of Galway Kinnell's,

> *The bud*
> *stands for all things,*

you may find, as I have, that they give you the feeling of wanting to live large again on the canvas of your life. For we, too, are buds, you and I, full of a life unfolding into flower. These two short lines stir the faith in me; faith in the potential that is inherent in everything. They make me believe in possibility again, in the promise of a great deal to come from the smallest of beginnings. For a bud pours into being by some miraculous volition from out of the womb of nowhere and nothing. Nothing seems to become something. And that is how it is for us, says Kinnell. But not just us. Everything starts out that way.

Kinnell strings the whole poem on one long, single sentence as if to mirror the thread of life, what is known in the Jewish tradition as the *Shma* ("Hear, O Israel, the Lord our God the Lord is One"). The one thread links the bud to the hand of Saint Francis, to the brow of the sow, to the teats, to the piglets below, to "all things." So even the form of this poem testifies to the unbroken connectedness of the stream of blessing. Kinnell wants us to recognize the blessedness of the entire spectrum of creation.

> *The bud*
> *stands . . .*
> *even for those things that don't flower,*
> *for everything flowers, from within, of self-blessing;*

A remarkable declaration. Some say that poetry is not the medium for delivering a message, that it should evoke by allusion, show rather than tell. But, Kinnell, like Mary Oliver, is willing to make bold statements without any apology. Everything, he says, comes into its own fullness through the process of self-blessing. In this sense, the bud can indeed stand for all things because even those that don't flower externally can do so from within. Now there is a vision of hope if ever there was one. And yet it is not only a matter of hope: to flower is the deepest intention of life itself. Without that intention, life would not even exist in the first place.

Everyone wants to feel the fullness of a life fully lived. The difference is in the strategy. Most think that fame and fortune will be their flowering. Others see their fruit to be in their family. Some strike out on wild adventures, while a few devote themselves to prayer and meditation. Whatever the method, the aim is fundamentally the same—to satisfy a longing for wholeness. We can chase many rainbows before we realize that what we truly want, however, lies in the one place we never thought to look. The flower of our life is already in bud even now, precisely in our present circumstances.

Galway Kinnell's beautiful, deeply compassionate poem suggests we look to ourselves for our flowering.

for everything flowers, from within, of self-blessing;

This line alone can turn your life around. It is poetry as revelation. I don't think the poet is saying that everything flowers, but that everything flowers from self-blessing. That's why it's not automatic. Not all of us know the blessing of that experience. He doesn't say self-love, which is open to different interpretations; he says self-blessing. A blessing is an act of reverence, usually freely given from one to another, and traditionally within some religious context or in a rite of passage. Here, Kinnell says that the deepest blessing comes from yourself. Like any other blessing, however, it is not a matter of will; of deciding to give yourself that gift. It arises, spontaneously, from the silence in you. Or not.

When a priest blesses his flock, he serves as a conduit for the stored spiritual power of his tradition. When a father blesses his son, he is passing on the blessings of his own father and his ancestral line. That flow of energy is the blessing. So a blessing, wherever it comes from, joins us to the larger body of life. It nourishes and heals us with sustenance from the invisible realms.

Blessings do not always come gift wrapped in gold. Usually some time after the event, we may speak of great misfortune as being a blessing in disguise. There is both a poetic and an etymological connection between our word *bless* and the French *blessure,* meaning "wound." Our wounds confer blessings on us when we embrace them as part of who we are, when we accept that the brightness of our fire also casts shadows. The wounded healer is one who has dived deep into his own vulnerability and sickness, and returned with the gift of compassion as well as a knowledge that can heal others.

Whichever way they appear, blessings give an experience of the world that is richer, more full of life and meaning, than the one we had known before. Like the feeling of emerging from cloud cover into an endless expanse of blue. Like a flood of warmth from the top of your head down to your toes. Or like the sensation of belonging, of realizing that you have your own unique place in the family of things. A blessing is an influx of grace.

And this, declares Galway Kinnell, is something that we give to ourselves. Kinnell is firmly in the lineage of Whitman, and nowhere more so than here.

There will soon be no more priests. Their work is
done. . . . Every man shall be his own priest.[1]

So said Whitman in *Song of Myself* in the 1850s. Forget the
notion of lineage and the traditional chain of command; just
apply for the direct connection. To apply, you have to ask,
not someone out there, but the truth of your own heart. You
open to the fact that every assistance you need, every kind of
knowing, both of the earth and the stars, is already reflected
down in the deep well of your being. All you need is to be
quiet enough not to make ripples in the reflection.

Kinnell, too, is sure of our capacity to minister blessings to
ourselves. You can look upon yourself in such a way that a
spring can break out in your heart. You can draw from the well
of wisdom that lies, mirrorlike, down in the depths of your
soul. To listen quietly and deeply to the stirrings of your own
life is already an act of self-blessing. To be kind to yourself. To
have faith that your life has its own intelligent design, that it is
doing exactly what it needs to, even if it doesn't feel that way:
that is a blessing. To know, though not with a cerebral knowing, that truth and beauty live in you: that, too, is a blessing.

> *though sometimes it is necessary*
> *to reteach a thing its loveliness,*
> *to put a hand on the brow*
> *of the flower*
> *and retell it in words and in touch*
> *it is lovely*
> *until it flowers again from within, of self-blessing;*

It is true that we don't feel the blessing of our life all the time, or even most of the time. This kind of love doesn't arise in us too often. Kinnell is saying that we forget our loveliness sometimes; and we can actually help each other remember by the way that we are in each other's presence. We can help one another; we can love one another this way. This is our saving grace: that, when we feel too far removed from ourselves to be able to feel how our life is already flowering, someone else can remind us how blessed we are. And this is what makes this poem a love poem.

If you have the genuine feeling that everyone, yourself as well as your lover, your child, your parents, even your enemies—everyone in your life—is already flowering from within, then the person you are with may feel that too and begin to remember for themselves their own truth and beauty. All it may need is a word or two, or a touch—for Kinnell knows, if anyone does, that the tangible body carries its own medicine.

You cannot "reteach a thing its loveliness" if your motive is to change another person. This would suggest that how they are is not good enough, and that you can do something about it. It is not in your power to enlighten another, make them better, or even bless them. All you can do is remind them, by your presence, of the flowering that they already are. Love is an environment more than a set of principles. An environment that, simply by existing, draws out another into his or her own fullness.

However good your principles and intentions may be, they won't reach far unless it is love itself that places your hand upon their brow. Then your hand will be light as a feather, unencumbered by the thought of trying to be of help, without any trace of wanting to make things different. Instead of platitudes, you will utter blessings, though your blessings will come not from you but from the stream of life that pours through you.

This is what Saint Francis does for the sow in Kinnell's poem. All of Kinnell's work is a celebration of this earthly life, and nothing is too lowly to be excluded from that praise. He celebrates the living beauty and sadness of this world. Of starfish, lovemaking, roots, and mud. And it is down into the humble mud of this earthly life that the second half of this poem brings us, down into the "fodder and slops" of the lumbering sow.

Of all animals, the pig is perhaps the most reviled. He carries a biblical curse. He is pronounced greedy and unclean, his flesh not even worthy of being eaten. We picture the pig, the sow, rolling in excrement, slobbering about in filth that no other self-respecting animal would dream of calling home. Yet it is precisely upon the "creased forehead" of this animal that Saint Francis lays his hand, and tells her,

blessings of the earth on the sow, . . .

The earth, in bringing the sow into being, is blessing her form and her life exactly as it is. Saint Francis is putting into words the implicit blessing of the earth that is present in the sow's very existence. If the earth had meant the sow to be

different, it would have done something about it. And so it is
with us.

This has to be the most exquisite appreciation of a sow
ever written. You sense her heaviness, the slime on her snout;
you can hear all the sucking and blowing of her offspring
below her, the spurting of her milk into their mouths.
Kinnell brings her so close you can almost smell the sweet
mustiness of her breath. He makes us feel an intimate of this
animal that others shun.

He helps us to feel that, like us—like everything—she
consists of both light and dark; she stretches all the way from
earthen snout to the spiritual curl of tail. See how Kinnell
draws the image of the cross here. First he traces the lateral
movement from snout to tail; then he follows the transverse
line down from the spine to the broken heart. This pig is on
the cross, bearing the weight of this earthly life as we all are.

Like many of us, too, she has a great broken heart.
Broken, perhaps, by the weight of the curses heaped upon
her since time began, by the lowliness that others have
foisted upon her, by the feelings of ugliness and self-loathing
that cling to her like a second skin. Some of us know how the
sow must feel.

She comes, despite all this, and through the blessing of
Saint Francis and the earth, to remember

the long, perfect loveliness of sow.

She remembers, not just in the sense of a memory recall,
but "all down her thick length"—in all the cells of her

body—that she is perfect exactly as she is, slops and all. Not that she is better than anyone else, or that she measures up to some external measure of perfection, but that her very existence is enough in itself to validate fully her being here. Being here just as she is, in her own unique "sow-ness." It is the felt sensation of her true beauty that flowers in the sow: and that is the blessing.

> *If we could blossom*
> *Out of ourselves, giving*
> *Nothing imperfect, withholding nothing!*

cries Denise Levertov in her poem "The Métier of Blossoming."[2] In Kinnell's world, that is exactly what the sow does, with the help of Saint Francis. The Franciscan blessing is the work of the true mentor, the healer, the guide. Perhaps you were blessed in this way by a teacher in your youth; or by someone who listened to you, believed in you, showed you your talent.

Notice, though, that it is not Saint Francis who gives the blessing, but the earth. The true guide knows that he does nothing of himself; that all blessings come from a source beyond himself. Ultimately, that source is in the person, or the pig, who is being reminded of the blessing he or she already is.

This is the love—and the loveliness—that we can extend to each other as well as to ourselves. Sometimes, through their books or works of art, we can receive blessings from those we have never met. This poem itself is such a hand on our brow.

4

LOVE AT FIRST SIGHT

by Wislawa Szymborska

They're both convinced
that a sudden passion joined them.
Such certainty is beautiful,
but uncertainty is more beautiful still.

Since they'd never met before, they're sure
that there'd been nothing between them.
But what's the word from the streets,
*   staircases, hallways—*
perhaps they've passed by each other a
*   million times?*

I want to ask them
if they don't remember—
a moment face to face
in some revolving door?
perhaps a "sorry" muttered in a crowd?
a curt "wrong number" caught in the receiver?—
but I know the answer.
No, they don't remember.

They'd be amazed to hear
that Chance has been toying with them
now for years.

Not quite ready yet
to become their Destiny,
it pushed them close, drove them apart,
it barred their path,
stifling a laugh,
and then leaped aside.

There were signs and signals,
even if they couldn't read them yet.
Perhaps, three years ago
or just last Tuesday
a certain leaf fluttered
from one shoulder to another?
Something was dropped and then picked up.
Who knows, maybe the ball that vanished
into childhood's thicket?

There were doorknobs and doorbells
where one touch had covered another
beforehand.
Suitcases, checked and standing side by side.
One night, perhaps, the same dream,
grown hazy by morning.

Every beginning
is only a sequel, after all,
and the book of events
is always open halfway through.

You Never Know

Wislawa Szymborska is one of the few women ever to have won the Nobel Prize for Literature. In her Nobel lecture, delivered on receiving the prize in 1996, Szymborska said that the inspiration of the poet is born more than anything else from a moment-by-moment attitude of "I don't know."

From this starting point, Szymborska suggested, everything becomes a source of wonder. Any poem, essay, or argument in response to the wondrous nature of the world must always be, at best, makeshift and, finally, inadequate. Perhaps all we can say, she concluded, is that nothing—but nothing—is ordinary.

If this is true of a stone or a cloud, a day of long rain, how true this must also be of the subject of love. Love, of all things, is something we cannot know the mind of. It envelops us; seizes us; not the other way around. The only thing we can be sure of is that its roots and branches stretch far and wide beyond our small horizon. So in this poem, Szymborska is challenging the assumption that love at first sight erupts out of nowhere.

As if a flame burst into existence without any kindling or tinder. That is how it felt to me when, as I describe in my reflections on the first poem in this book, my gaze met that of the woman across the room when I was thirty. Because it took me completely by surprise, I assumed it just happened, as if by some fateful accident. Perhaps I hadn't seen the clues that were there all along. Who is to say?

This poem urges us to ask the question, not to come up with answers. It invites us to allow the possibility that our lives were never entirely in our hands, if indeed at all. Of all things, love is the greatest mystery. Better, then, not to hold fast to certainties about where it came from or where it might lead; to fixed ideas about how vulnerable or protected we may be in the face of love's arrows. Love strikes the most unlikely targets, and leaves other, apparently likely candidates unscathed.

The lovers in Szymborska's poem are convinced that, since they had never met before, there had been nothing between them previously. That's only logical, after all. But Szymborska asks us to suspend our judgment and ready assumptions. For all they know, they may have crossed each other's paths a million times and not noticed. Think of all those chance and fleeting encounters with a stranger you may have had in the past year. Who was that person who dialed your number by mistake? Why your number and not your neighbor's?

Standing in an elevator with a crowd of anonymous faces, coming out of a door as someone else is coming in, bumping into someone on the street: for the poetic imagination, these are not irrelevant trifles with no bearing on your day. For the poet, there is no such thing as normal, no such thing as an ordinary event. Especially, perhaps, for someone like Szymborska, who, like her contemporary Czeslaw Milosz, is Polish and has lived through a constant series of upheavals and devastations in her country. "Nothing is usual or normal," Szymborska concluded in her Nobel lecture.

Which means, not that we are always wanting to squeeze some meaning and significance out of any given moment in a day, but that we are open to the possibility that life is happening right now in a way that stretches far beyond all our knowing. That kind of innocence can open the door to a larger life than we could ever dream of.

I see now, with the benefit of hindsight, how a meeting in a revolving door did in fact lead, a year later, to my sitting down at a lunch table opposite the woman who is now my wife. In 1997, I was in Boulder, Colorado, researching a book on spirituality in America. Before attending a conference there on spirituality in education, I had an appointment at 6 P.M. to meet a couple in the lobby of the Boulderado Hotel. We had never met before, and I told them that I was sometimes mistaken for Ken Wilber, the bald-headed and somewhat reclusive writer who lives in Boulder who was an acquaintance of theirs.

At 6 P.M. I came through the revolving door of the hotel to be greeted by a woman who beamed at me. "Ken!" she smiled. "Hello!" I grinned, imagining she was joking about the comparison I had made between myself and the writer. We shook hands, our free hands resting momentarily on each other's shoulders. Then she looked at me quizzically for a second.

"It is Ken, isn't it?" she said, only half in the manner of a question.

"Sure," I laughed. "Is your husband here, too?"

She stopped. "Ken Wilber. I'm waiting for Ken Wilber. We are meant to be meeting here at six. I'm so sorry, I thought you were him."

We excused ourselves, and then went off to find our respective dates. The next day, at the conference, I again bumped into the woman I had met at the revolving door. She turned out to be the wife of the president of a funding organization in Michigan with a private retreat facility. Over the course of the conference, we got to know each other, and she introduced me to her husband. When I told him about my book, he offered me the use of their retreat facility for a month of writing time.

A year later, I accepted his offer. Just before leaving for Michigan, his office called me and said they had double-booked for the first ten days of my retreat, so they had found me a room for those days in another retreat center that was just over the hill. It was a Christian Mennonite center. I had never heard of the Mennonites, but all I needed was a quiet place to write, so I thanked them, and a few days later was walking through the front door of a converted barn in the middle of hay fields. The following day, I went downstairs for lunch, which was in silence. There was a long refectory table with an elderly couple at one end and someone else at the far end. My place was laid opposite the other guest's.

I took my food, and sat down in my place. Then I looked up, and beheld one of the most beautiful faces I have ever seen. The woman's large eyes rested on me with a radiant smile. I looked down at my food and glanced up again. Her gaze was still on me, showering me with a direct, uncomplicated warmth. The whole room seemed to fill with her presence. I tried not to laugh. The Mennonites were eating their dessert, oblivious. I was filled with disbelief, incomprehension, and inexpressible joy. Maria had booked into the retreat center for the exact ten days I was there. We were the only guests. Two years later, we were married.

> *They'd be amazed to hear*
> *that Chance has been toying with them*
> *now for years.*

It is hard not to conclude that Maria and I met due to some larger design; we might even go so far as to adopt the story that we had known each other many times in previous lives. It certainly felt like that; though in reality, I simply don't know. And I agree with Szymborska: the uncertainty is more beautiful still. All I know is that when my eyes looked up, I was met by a gaze that I found deeply familiar. When she saw me, Maria tells me that she recognized me instantly. She knew me, somehow.

Where do these intuitions come from? We are so keen to interpret the mysteries of the world. The mind likes to settle for one answer or another. But to stay open to the possibility, to feel the experience, whatever it is, without nailing it down with a plausible explanation; that is a more difficult, yet, I believe, a richer, deeper response.

It seems to me that in this poem, Szymborska is not so much telling us what always happens when two lovers meet; she is wanting to make room for the completely implausible. She is breathing new life into the ancient story that some people are meant for each other. By design, this story goes, such people will unknowingly be in search of each other across time and space. It's a myth at least as old as Plato, and one that is at the very heart of romantic love. You may scoff at the idea; you may have years of proof that such things don't happen. But what do *we* know? this poem asks.

If the story has survived for so long, it is because it gives voice to the longing deep within the hearts of so many women and men. My own inclination is to describe that longing as the archetypal wish for union with God, with Life itself. But again, what do I know? Whatever our explanations, the longing itself is genuine, a fact of being human, whether the story we clothe it in is true or false.

The poem reminds us that there is a season and a time for things that cannot be orchestrated. It's like death—when it's our time, we fall. Lovers need to ripen on the vine. You will know the right moment by the ease with which you fall into this next chapter of your life. It will require no effort, just an assenting to what wants to happen.

Through the whole poem, Szymborska is opening our eyes to the possibility—the probability—that our life is not in our control, that life arranges things as in a dance, like the whirling of the atoms, in which every particle has its own unique place and orbit. Those orbits cross when the symmetry of the dance as a whole makes it desirable. Imagine what that means! That there is nothing to contrive, nothing to try to make happen! We don't have to try to orchestrate life. It is already in hand. What a relief it would be if we could live life this way.

This is not a passive, but an open response to life. It doesn't suggest we don't do anything, or make any effort. It doesn't even mean it is senseless to go to a dating agency. It suggests we do what we do because we are moved to do so, not because we are trying to manipulate life to fit our expectations. Everything is in the motivation. Open to the dance, fling off the cloak of cynicism—of seeing life to be a repetition of how it has always been—and you will enter the simplicity of not knowing, arms open wide to life. In that condition (not a negative state, but a condition of accessibility), the intelligence of life will call your tune and lead you where you long to go, even though it may look very different from anything you ever imagined.

Wislawa Szymborska brings her poem to a close with four lines that can send tremors through anyone's bloodstream. Try it, read them out loud:

> *Every beginning*
> *is only a sequel, after all,*
> *and the book of events*
> *is always open halfway through.*

This is the vision of life that you can glimpse through the whole poem. Our life is an ongoing story, every sentence and word following the previous page and leading to the next. Neither is the author who we think we are. No need to worry, then, if you think you have lost the plot. Love, and do what you will, Saint Augustine said. For everything is already well, and just as it needs to be.

5

LOVE

by Czeslaw Milosz

Love means to look at yourself
The way one looks at distant things
For you are only one thing among many.
And whoever sees that way heals his heart,
Without knowing it, from various ills—
A bird and a tree say to him: Friend.

Then he wants to use himself and things
So that they stand in the glow of ripeness.
It doesn't matter whether he knows what he serves:
Who serves best doesn't always understand.

One Among Many

"*Love is at first not anything that means merging, giving over, and uniting with another. . . . It is a high inducement to the individual to ripen, to become something in himself, to become world, to become world for himself for another's sake.*"

RAINER MARIA RILKE,
On Love and Other Difficulties[1]

This poem by Czeslaw Milosz echoes the ripening that Rilke speaks of. Instead of looking outside of ourselves for love, he counsels looking back at ourselves; but in a very particular way,

The way one looks at distant things . . .

How do we look at distant things? We see in perspective when we see from afar. We see things in context, as part of a larger picture. If we can look at ourselves in this way, we may see that we are only one among many. That others have their troubles, too, their own stories, their own fears and aspirations. There is a relief in this way of seeing. It siphons away the pressure of self-preoccupation, and encourages us to look up, to lift our gaze and become aware that other living beings inhabit this world. Think of the lines by Mary Oliver in her poem "Wild Geese":

> *Tell me about despair, yours. I will tell you mine.*
> *Meanwhile the world goes on.*[2]

A realization like this can generate kindness, not to mention humility. *Humility, humus, humor*—they all come from the same linguistic root, which means "of the earth." Humility brings us down to earth, and allows us the latitude to laugh at ourselves. Self-preoccupation, on the other hand, is a serious matter. It surrounds us in such a cloud of our own preconceptions that we cannot see anyone else, much less learn to love them.

If nothing else, the course of history probably shocked Milosz out of any excess of self-preoccupation. He has lived a long life. He was born in Lithuania in 1911 of Polish-speaking parents, and was brought up in Poland. He witnessed the Russian Revolution, the First and Second World Wars, the rise and fall of Stalin and Communism. He has known often what it is like to trudge down a road with the city that had been home a smoking ruin behind him. He defected from the Soviet Bloc to Paris in 1951, became a professor of Slavic languages and literature at Berkeley in 1961, and won the Nobel Prize for Literature in 1980. Joseph Brodsky, the Russian poet, said that Milosz is "one of the greatest, if not the greatest, poet of our time."

If anyone has been given the historical perspective with which to see himself, as well as the course of events in general, from a certain distance, it is Czeslaw Milosz. This, I suspect, along with a lifelong inclination toward all that lies beyond appearances, has helped to shape the wisdom and the beauty that flowers in this poem.

Milosz says that this other, more detached way of seeing will heal your heart. The ills that distance can heal for us must include the double bind of Narcissus, the youth who found it so difficult to break away from the love of his own image in the water. A narcissist—again, I speak with some degree of personal experience—tends to see others as characters in his own story, and the world as his stage. "Look at me!" he cries, strutting up and down his own particular patch. "Pay attention to me! Listen to my troubles, my triumphs, my views. Don't disturb me and don't interrupt."

When my only son was a child, I was strongly attached to not being woken early (I still have the same attachment). I was also very attached to my morning meditation practice. So when my son would wake up, I would make it clear that he needed to slip quietly into the family room and stay there playing on his own until after I had finished my meditation. The obvious—that he was alone, and probably lonely—seemed to pass me right by. My habits were more important to me than my son feeling loved. Occasionally, I would leap up out of meditation and call to him to be quiet, the irony almost completely lost on me. That is self-absorption; and it is not pretty.

You may know people like this (we are everywhere). We are as likely to be introverted as extroverted. There are many ways to claim attention and fill up a stage. Some are able to do it without saying a word—just by exuding an atmosphere of "poor me," the unfortunate victim of circumstance. Whatever the tactic, Narcissus is so self-involved that it is impossible for him to realize that there are others who inhabit this world with equal claim to him. As long as the narcissistic wound continues to call our tune, we are essentially incapable of love. For love requires enough spaciousness to include others, to value them, and to feel their pain and joys as much as our own.

When you live from the nonattachment Milosz advises— the nonattachment to the idea of being special—you heal your heart "without knowing it." The healing happens of its own accord, unself-consciously. Things just fall away. One of the things that falls away is self-consciousness. Narcissus is acutely aware of himself at all times because he fills his own screen. There is nothing else to be aware of.

Milosz speaks here not just to the alleviation of narcissism but to its ultimate healing. To be so open to the world that, like Saint Francis, other beings begin speaking to you in a language you can understand. You feel the heart of all beings, and through your own heart those beings speak to you and call you friend. They call you friend because you yourself exude friendship. As the sense of being somebody special— somebody deserving of special treatment and attention—falls away, the sense of belonging increases proportionately.

Isn't that a strange thing, that distance—nonattachment— actually increases our sense of belonging? The term *nonattachment* is easily misunderstood. It may sound as if it implies a disconnection from things and events, as if the

world can tumble about us and we can remain unmoved, seeing it from afar as if it were the inevitable workings of karma
that people and things have brought upon themselves. But
no, that is the shadow of nonattachment, which is a defen-
siveness born of the fear of intimacy. That kind of detach-
ment sees everything else as essentially other; and it can lead
only to alienation and isolation.

The distance that Milosz describes gives rise to love. The
nonattachment that the Buddhists value so highly flowers
into loving-kindness. It is a distance first and foremost from
yourself; in the sense that it no longer continually places you
at center stage. When you are no longer center stage, you
can allow others to breathe alongside you; you can appreciate their existence as being equal in value to your own.

No longer the star in your own movie, you can feel a kinship with others that naturally gives rise to a sense of belonging. Living beings are no longer other; they are part of you,
and you share in their joys and tribulations, whoever they
are, however different to you they may appear to be. Nonattachment does not mean you do not suffer; it may even
mean that you suffer more deeply. But your suffering will not
turn you in on yourself; it will turn you outward, to the
world. To suffer with: this is the meaning of compassion.

Saint Francis was a rare case. Like a few others scattered
through history, he underwent a night of transformation in
which he died to his old self and emerged from the ashes a new
human being, the friend of everything that lived and breathed.
The mirror was broken and he became forever free of the
tyranny of his own image. More commonly, the loosening of

the narcissistic fixation happens by degrees, and the dying of the old Adam is usually a lifetime's journey along a painful, though rewarding, road. "To ripen, to become something in himself, to become world, to become world for himself for another's sake"—this is love's road, in Rilke's words.

Part of the radiance, the beauty of this poem by Czeslaw Milosz, is that it holds up such a clear image of the possible. Not that we have to be there in a single night of the phoenix, but that this is what is possible for us as human beings, at any moment. Love is the promise of our kind, that we may be in this world in such a way that everything with which we come into contact is offered a respect, a reverence, even, which furthers the glow of its ripeness. Echoes of Rilke again.

When Milosz speaks of using

> *himself and things*
> *So that they stand in the glow of ripeness*

I do not think he means that we have to do something in particular. Milosz, like Rilke, is anything but a utilitarian. He is not urging us to go out and do self-conscious charitable acts in the hope of helping others to grow. No, it is enough to be a presence of that love wherever we are; an environment in which, without any conscious intent of being of use or not, others can flower.

That unself-consciousness is both our fundamental innocence and also our protection. It protects us from claiming our virtue—our love—as our own. Love serves, not because it thinks it is a good thing to do, but because it can't help itself. With no separation between the one loving and the one being loved, there is only love, being itself. Easy to say; may you and I have the great good fortune to be struck one day by such a life-giving arrow. This poem shows us how to become a likely target. When that happens, love will be all that remains.

6

KINDNESS

by Naomi Shihab Nye

Before you know what kindness really is
you must lose things,
feel the future dissolve in a moment
like salt in a weakened broth.
What you held in your hand,
what you counted and carefully saved,
all this must go so you know
how desolate the landscape can be
between the regions of kindness.
How you ride and ride
thinking the bus will never stop,
the passengers eating maize and chicken
will stare out the window forever.

Before you learn the tender gravity of kindness,
you must travel where the Indian in a white poncho
lies dead by the side of the road.

You must see how this could be you,
how he too was someone
who journeyed through the night with plans
and the simple breath that kept him alive.

Before you know kindness as the deepest thing inside,
you must know sorrow as the other deepest thing.
You must wake up with sorrow.
You must speak to it till your voice
catches the thread of all sorrows
and you see the size of the cloth.

Then it is only kindness that makes any sense anymore,
only kindness that ties your shoes
and sends you out into the day to mail letters and
   purchase bread,
only kindness that raises its head
from the crowd of the world to say
It is I you have been looking for,
and then goes with you everywhere
like a shadow or a friend.

It Is You I Have Been Looking For

In my response to the first poem in this book, I recall my experience of falling in love for the first time. When, a few months later, the tide of life pulled the two of us apart, everything else fell away as well. My work ended; all the friends and colleagues I had spent days and nights with for years suddenly stopped calling. Even my name was no longer mentioned in that circle. I had been one of the spokespersons for a spiritual group that was well known in London at the time ("You are young. So you know everything."), and it shook the foundations of the organization when I fell in love with the wife of another of the group's leaders. In a matter of weeks, I lost my source of income, my friends, whatever reputation I had, and the woman who had opened the eyes of my heart.

> *Before you know what kindness really is*
> *you must lose things,*
> *feel the future dissolve in a moment*
> *like salt in a weakened broth.*

The pain and the shame of being an outcast was compounded by the prospect of never seeing that woman again. My heart went numb for what seemed an eternity. In calendar time, it was perhaps a year. During that period, I was unaware of any increase of kindness toward others on my part. I felt dry as a desert well in summer. Nothing, not even loss, comes with a guarantee of some redeeming factor. Loss can close, as well as open, the heart. At that time, what kicked in was not kindness, but my survival mechanisms. I had to get off my butt and make a life and a living, not only for myself (for I, too, was married at the time) but also for my wife and child.

By the time my first marriage had ended, and another long-term relationship had also dissolved, life had had twenty-two years to do its work on me. I was no longer shielded in the same way from hurt. Sometime during the final months of that long-term love, I came out of a hotel in Washington just as a homeless person was trudging past with a sack on his back, stooped, his eyes hugging the ground. I stood on the forecourt and burst into tears, filled with his loneliness, my own, the loneliness of all of us. I wanted to run after him, empty my pockets for him, tell him I understood, which of course I mostly didn't.

He seemed so close, so dear to me in that fleeting moment, though at the time I stood and watched him go by, crying all the while, sensing that no response was more necessary than my own crumbling heart. This time, I could feel it, I needed to stay with my brokenness, not cover it over with a protective sheen. My brokenness was awakening me to a kinship with others I had never known so deeply before.

In this rending yet redemptive poem, Naomi Shihab Nye reaches down to the roots of our humanity, which lie in the great heart where we all cry together. Nye, an Arab American, has been writing poetry since she was five. She has published six books of poetry and several children's books. Born of a Palestinian father and an American mother, she has lived her life between those two cultures.

Her poem was sent to me by e-mail soon after the tragedy of September 11, 2001. With its unique ability to capture the significance of what the ordinary imagination cannot grasp, poetry took on a heightened value for the culture during those dark weeks. Poems circulated all over the Internet. As Nye said in her own e-mail response to the tragedy, "A Letter to Any Would-Be Terrorist," "poetry humanizes us in a way that news, or even religion, has a harder time doing."

> *you must lose things,*

What is it we have to lose? "Choose carefully/all you are going to lose, though any of it would do," says the poet Jane Hirshfield.[1] Any loss will do; anything, that is, that will help us see our kinship with every other living being. None of us has any firm ground beneath our feet. We are all on our way to the exit door. Recently, I have begun to feel my age. I have begun to feel differently about death, closer to it, than I did even five years ago. My memory, I have noticed, is not what it was. My bones ache a little, which they never did. My face carries a few age spots now.

Not long ago, I helped organize the move of my mother

into a nursing home. Once, she used to enjoy walks in the English countryside, and even a year ago, loved to travel to distant lands. She enjoyed literature and conversation. Now a stroke has confined her to a wheelchair, to a single room. Her eyes are fading fast, her memory is a dotted line. Now, when I see old people hesitantly climbing some steps, stooped on a cane, or navigating a ramp in a wheelchair, my heart goes out to them. Their struggle is my mother's, and through her, my own.

> *What you held in your hand,*
> *what you counted and carefully saved,*
> *all this must go so you know*
> *how desolate the landscape can be*
> *between the regions of kindness.*

What we count on and nurture all of our lives is our own continuity, and that of the people nearest to us. Nye is urging us in this poem to open our hearts to the fact that everything we cherish will pass out of our lives, and that we, too, shall pass away. When we come to know this truth as a lived experience, we shall also know a deep love and kindness for everyone else who must take the same road. Our pain, our suffering, does not make us special; on the contrary, it joins us to the human race.

Anna Swir, a Polish poet whose work has been translated by Czeslaw Milosz and Leonard Nathan, wrote a remarkable love poem called "The Same Inside." In it, she tells how she

was on her way to her lover when she passed a beggar woman
on the street.

> *I took her hand,*
> *kissed her delicate cheek,*
> *we talked, she was*
> *the same inside as I am,*
> *from the same kind,*
> *I sensed this instantly*
> *as a dog knows by scent*
> *another dog.*[2]

Swir could not part from the old woman, such love did she
feel for her out there in the rain. Soon, she realized she no
longer had any reason to go to her lover's place.

It was *bodhicitta* that emerged in Anna Swir that night—
the great beating heart of compassion that the Buddhists say
exists naturally in all beings, as sweetness pervades the pear.
When we no longer shield ourselves from the vulnerability of
our condition, when we feel the basic fragility of our existence, then we feel our essential identity with all living things.
Then compassion (literally, "to suffer with") arises naturally
for ourselves and for all others.

Naomi Shihab Nye leads us into a foreign country where
an Indian lies dead by the side of the road. Nye lives in San
Antonio, Texas, and is poetry editor for the *Texas Observer.*
She has a passion to illumine in her work the essential humanity of peoples misunderstood or feared by the mainstream.

You will often hear the voices of Mexican Americans, as well as those of the Middle East, in her poetry.

The man lying dead in a white poncho could also be you, she says. His skin color may be different, his clothing, too. But the dreams you have, the plans for tomorrow and the next day—he, like you, had his own. As did every one of those young Afghanis whose bodies lay strewn not so very long ago over the dry rocks around Kandahar. We all breathe the same breath, we all journey through our own form of night. "The tender gravity of kindness"—what a beautiful, many-layered phrase that is—knows no boundaries of caste or creed.

Yet it is not always easy to identify with peoples from far-away lands, who seem to live such different lives from our own, with other values than the ones we cherish. It can even be the case that we learn of their country's existence and place on the map only when our own country goes to war with them. It is easier to see our reflection closer to home; in the Xeroxed faces, for example, that papered the streets of Manhattan in the wake of the collapse of the World Trade Center. There we could not fail to see the precious, heart-breaking reflection of our own mortality.

The Tibetans have a simple practice that can help us feel this tenderness for others of any color or creed, whoever they may be. They call it *tonglen.* You breathe in the pain of the person you are thinking of, filling your lungs with that stream of darkness. Then you breathe out warmth and light in their direction, with the wish for them to be free of pain. Whenever you feel happiness, you breathe it out to others. When you feel your own pain, breathe it in and breathe out light, with the wish for everyone to be free of suffering. What we reject out there is only, after all, what we reject in ourselves; and the most numbing pain comes from the protected heart.

> *Before you know kindness as the deepest thing inside,*
> *you must know sorrow as the other deepest thing.*
> *You must wake up with sorrow.*
> *You must speak to it till your voice*
> *catches the thread of all sorrows*
> *and you see the size of the cloth.*

Maria, my wife, knows the sorrow of losing her three-year-old daughter to cancer. From the moment of diagnosis, a year before her death, Maria knew Hannah would die, even though the doctors said there was a chance of survival. For a year, on and off, she slept in the hospital with Hannah, holding her hand through all the possible treatments, with the intuition that Hannah would not live till her fourth birthday. When Hannah finally died, a few days before the beginning of her fourth year, Maria knew that she had nothing else to lose in her life. Nothing more dear could be taken away from her.

Stripped of everything, she slowly began to recognize a freedom in the midst of her sorrow. The approval of others no longer mattered; she knew she had to live, in her own unique way, this one life that was her own. She owed that not only to herself, but also to Hannah. Instead of closing down, her heart opened wide to the sorrow and pain of everyone.

This was Hannah's gift to Maria, and it became the title of the book she wrote of her story.[3]

Years later, we were driving down Fillmore Street in San Francisco. Suddenly Maria bent over, her head on her knees. When I asked her what was wrong, she said that she had just seen a man crying across the street while he was on the public telephone. His pain had entered her, and she was praying for him. Maria is one who has caught "the thread of all sorrows"; she sees "the size of the cloth."

This is the downward, rather than the upward, spiritual path. You go down, down into your own sorrow and suffering. Not indulgently, not milking your pain to consolidate yet another identity, but with a gesture of moment-by-moment openness to the reality of your condition—the condition of all of us. The "tender gravity of kindness" that emerges in this descent gives rise to a love that cannot die. For such a love is given freely from the depths of existence and can never be taken away.

Then it is only kindness that makes any sense anymore.

There will come a time when we do not need to commit conscious acts of loving kindness because we shall recognize that everything we do is cut from that cloth. When the heart has become an open door, kindness is the air we breathe and goes with us everywhere. Then, Naomi Shihab Nye tells us in her poem, we shall discover that this was what we were looking for all along, the elemental love that is who we are.

7

THE ACHE
OF MARRIAGE

by Denise Levertov

The ache of marriage:

thigh and tongue, beloved,
are heavy with it,
it throbs in the teeth

We look for communion
and are turned away, beloved,
each and each

It is leviathan and we
in its belly
looking for joy, some joy
not to be known outside it

two by two in the ark of
the ache of it.

A Hidden Joy

Most of the poems in this book praise the joys and beauties of love: its tenderness and kindness; its sense of destiny, the way it lifts us out of ourselves into a greater communion with the world at large. This poem will take you down into the depths instead of up into an open sky. These depths are good; they are thick with the dark leaves of many years, and in them lies the treasure worth digging for.

In marriage lie a treasure and a joy that can be found nowhere else—that is the paradoxical mystery and promise of this poem whose title, "The Ache of Marriage," suggests something quite different. Perhaps it is the faint knowledge of that hidden gold that leads so many of us still to enter its gates, even in a time when most marriages dissolve in a few years, and when, even in the process of getting married, many of us remain (understandably) cynical about the institution itself.

Marriage does not have a great reputation. It can get messy, and it is always shadowed by trials and troubles. Like a mortgage, it locks us in, if not for the duration, at least for the short term.

Don't lock me in wedlock, I want
marriage, an
encounter—

wrote Levertov in another of her poems, "About Marriage."[1]

Denise Levertov was herself married for much of her life to Mitchell Goodman, an American writer. She was born into a highly literate household in Wales, in 1923. When she was just twelve, she sent some of her poems to T. S. Eliot, who responded with two pages of "excellent advice" and encouragement to continue writing. She married Goodman in 1947, and they moved to the United States in 1948. Within a few years, the American literary community saw her as one of their own, and one of the outstanding poets of her time.

In her 1984 essay, "A Poet's View," Levertov said that "the acknowledgment and celebration of mystery probably constitutes the most consistent theme of my poetry."[2] Yet for Levertov, the mystery was to be found in the natural and internal worlds—in her own responses to the events of everyday life rather than in some transcendent vision. She saw love and marriage to be part of that mystery.

Marriage commits into form whatever love we have for another person, and in so doing, it joins us to the passage of time. It takes our winged feet, holds them on the ground, and binds us at the ankles to the one we have chosen. Anything that finds its way into form is subject to the scrapes and dents that come with time. Marriage is no exception, and the traditional Christian wedding vows—"for better for worse, for richer for poorer, in sickness and in health"—spell it out: not everything we sign up for is going to make us happy.

So why bother? Why do we do this to ourselves and to each other? Rilke was one of Denise Levertov's earliest mentors, and he had a good answer to that.

> Like so many other things, people have also mis-understood the position love has in life; they have made it into play and pleasure because they thought that play and pleasure are more blissful than work; but there is nothing happier than work, and love, precisely because it is the supreme happiness, can be nothing other than work.[3]

In another letter, he says,

> It is also good to love: because love is difficult. For one human being to love another human being: that is perhaps the most difficult task that has been entrusted to us, the ultimate task, the final test and proof, the work for which all other work is merely preparation.[4]

There is an ache in marriage that goes with the territory. You stand up before your community and publicly acknowl-edge your responsibility toward this form—"this ark," Denise Levertov calls it later in the poem—that joins you with another human being within the constraints of time. To acknowledge your place in time is to surrender the fantasy of immortality and limitless possibilities. It is to admit to the limits and gravity of the earth, to the wear and tear of life with feet of clay. Marriage, like every other form, will collect its own dents and scrapes along the way.

Levertov locates the ache of marriage specifically in the thigh, the tongue, and the teeth. The thigh: sexual love is shadowed with its own lingering pain, she implies. In making love, we are at our most vulnerable and open, most susceptible to hurt, intended or otherwise. When you marry, though, the ache may be compounded by the bond of monogamy. When you feel estranged from your spouse, angry, or fearful, you are still bound by the promise to join body and soul with your spouse alone.

You may long for your lovemaking to take you "higher than wine," while in reality "meat and potatoes love" is your usual fare (as Alicia Ostriker observes so graphically in her own poem "Wanting All").[5] You may ache for more rapturous lovemaking, and you may long to look elsewhere. But in marriage, you have set yourself the limit of being with one person, so if you are to honor those limits, you must undertake the work of forging a deeper intimacy, as well as a deeper relationship with your own disappointment. This is the work of love that Rilke refers to.

How deep is the sorrow that can be caused by the tongue. Days, weeks, even years after a hurtful word, you may still feel the ache of it beneath your ribs. Your spouse may set your teeth on edge the way a knife does when it scrapes over a plate. Just by the way he slops coffee on the kitchen counter; by his righteousness about the state of the world, about people who don't share his political views; by the way he says he loves you, grudgingly somehow, and only when you have said it first.

In marriage there is no escape from the dark corners of another human being. There is no escape from the mirror another casts on my own sorry state. However exalted my intentions—however ready I am to quote some spiritual wisdom from some great author or text—marriage, by design, offers me a context in which to see through the mirage of my own defenses. It summons into awareness the fears, the resentments, the disillusion, the sheer difficulty that comes with the fact of being human.

Perhaps this is not the picture we thought we signed up for. We may choose to live for years without seeing what is before our eyes, without our shell cracking open to allow the wellspring of some deeper love to flow through our days. After all, it requires sorrow, as well as joy, for those waters to flow; the sorrow of recognizing one's own loveless state, one's own rigid stance toward the other and the world.

I lived in that prison of my own making for ten years or more in my first marriage. I did not know what love is. And I ascribed much of my ignorance to my wife's own protected heart, without ever coming to the humbling realization that the darkness lay in my own eyes, not in hers. How could I be the one who was lacking in love? I was the one (it seemed to me) with the insight and information. I was the one who could talk about the meaning of life and convey a semblance of authority. I squirm now even to look at these words on the page. But it's the truth. And I didn't know any better. Life hadn't broken me open yet.

No one I know of has captured our imperfection in words as poignantly as Robert Bly in these lines from his poem "Listening to the Köln Concert":

> *The inner nest, not made by instinct*
> *Will never be quite round,*
> *And each has to enter the nest*
> *Made by the other, imperfect bird.*[6]

In the same poem, Bly says that marriage calls us to abandon our longing for the perfect; for our partner's perfection, and also for our own. As we open to our own imperfections, we can begin to have mercy on those of others. Our imperfections, after all, are what join us to the human race. In letting our frailty be part of our experience of ourselves without judgment or criticism—it's the way things are, after all—we may begin to know compassion, both for ourselves and the world. The willingness to live with eyes open, fearing neither what you will see in the other nor what they will see in you— this is part of the savage grace that is marriage.

> *We look for communion*
> *and are turned away, beloved,*
> *each and each*

How close to the marrow these lines are, evoking as they do our perpetual aloneness. Throughout her poem, Denise Levertov never ceases to call her husband "beloved." Even in the anguish of longing for communion with him and always being turned away—not by her husband, but by the fact that they will forever be separate individuals, however close they come to each other—even so, he remains her beloved.

This is the ebb and flow of intimacy—we draw close, and we pull away, because we are always subject to the eternal dance of wanting to dissolve into union and, at the same time, to affirm our individuality. In the excerpt quoted on page 80 from another of her poems, Levertov says that marriage is an encounter, not a merging. An encounter requires two people. It calls for a separateness-in-togetherness. Even so, there is an ache in the realization that, "even between the closest people infinite distances exist." (Rilke)[7]

After my first marriage, I lived with a woman for twelve years. It was with her that I first learned to love, and came to see love as a true work. We never married, perhaps because we had both been married before and were wary. But twelve years is a long wariness by anyone's standards. No, our avoidance of marriage went deeper than past disappointments. I think we knew somehow from the very beginning that even this relationship, too, would pass.

Yet we would say, only half in jest, that we were twin souls. We spoke the same language, had similar responses to the world around us, even had similar body movements and gestures. It was as if we were two pieces of the same puzzle. Her presence would sometimes feel as close to me as my own body, mingled in with my own life stream. For the first few years, our days were often full of laughter, levity, and a shared love of silence.

The trouble with twin souls, however, is that they can offer each other no reflection. There is only one of them, the classic narcissistic bind. In reaction to this, we would pull away from each other and retreat into our respective projects, declaring that our relationship existed to mutually inspire each other in our respective work and place in the world. At the same time, we would clothe our love for each other in lofty jargon, which helped to veil its more basic instinct of self-preservation.

For twelve years we tussled with the tension of separateness-in-togetherness. We needed to forge our own ways, yet we needed each other for support and approval. Like so many couples, of course. Except we were never able to harmonize fully these two different (and legitimate) needs. One of us would feel compromised if we began giving too much attention to the other's endeavors; then the other would feel neglected. We used to joke that we needed a wife to look after us both. What we called the feeling of being twin souls, a professional might call codependence. The truth, perhaps, lay somewhere in between.

Finally, we had to pull ourselves apart in order to become whole in ourselves. Life was ready to break us open, and break open we did. In *The Prophet*, Kahlil Gibran writes,

*For even as love crowns you, so shall he crucify you. Even
as he is for your growth so is he for your pruning.*[8]

You might say—and I tend to believe this—that our parting was in the design all along, which does not mean it
diminished the richness we knew together. It was woven into
our first meeting in the intuition that this would not be forever. Somehow, we always know these things, even if we
don't want to know. In the same way that when I watched
Maria drive away from that retreat house, I knew, though it
made no sense whatsoever, that she would become my wife.
I, who felt entirely unfit for yet another relationship, and
who had always looked rather disparagingly on the institution, suddenly knew that marriage was to be the culmina-
tion of my experience of intimacy. And it was stunningly
simple.

When you know there is absolutely nothing else for you to
do, it is simple to walk down into the belly of the whale.
There was no doubt in my heart that I would walk that road
with Maria, though my mind continued for some while to
dredge up all manner of anxieties and rational arguments to
persuade me to the contrary. There is a joy down there,
down in the belly of commitment, "not to be known outside
it," Levertov says. It took me fifty-three years and a whole lot
of grace to learn she was right.

I am too new to the joys of marriage to make any pro-
nouncements. But I know that what flows in my veins is a
quiet joy now. It brings me to rest. Though from the very first

moment Maria and I felt we knew each other in an intimate, even ancient way, the description of soul twins never applied. Our otherness, I am finding, is a rich, and sometimes challenging, vein.

Marriage is indeed an ark, and one in which the very ache of being human can be redeemed through acceptance. In some ways, I am as much of a fool as I ever was, but in this ark, my foolishness does not belittle me in my own eyes as once it did. My wife has her imperfections, too, but I am learning to see that the phantoms they raise spring from my own darkness as much as from hers.

Finally, I am beginning to feel for myself the quiet elation—and the breath, the breath—in the lines of Rilke that follow on from his speaking of the infinite distances between people. When a couple accepts their essential otherness, he says (when they enter "the ark of / the ache of it," in Levertov's spectacular phrase),

> a marvelous living side-by-side can grow up for them, if they succeed in loving the expanse between them, which gives them the possibility of always seeing each other as a whole and before an immense sky.[9]

I know that to be true now. As for the ache, it is my experience that its value can be credited to the next account, if, like me, you ever have the uncertain honor of having traveled the road of serial monogamy, married or otherwise. I doubt I would have been ready for my current marriage if I had not been broken open beforehand; and if another woman hadn't already given years to sharing the rocky road of love with me. When I look back over a lifetime of intimate relationships, those heartwarming words of the great Spanish poet Antonio Machado spring to my mind:

> *The golden bees are making sweet honey*
> *From all my old failures.*[10]

8

LOVE SONNET LXXXIX

by Pablo Neruda

When I die, I want your hands on my eyes:
I want the light and wheat of your beloved hands
to pass their freshness over me once more:
I want to feel the softness that changed my destiny.

I want you to live while I wait for you, asleep.
I want your ears still to hear the wind, I want you
to sniff the sea's aroma that we loved together,
to continue to walk on the sand we walk on.

I want what I love to continue to live
and you whom I love and sang above everything else
to continue to flourish, full-flowered:

so that you can teach everything my love directs
    you to,
so that my shadow can travel along in your hair,
so that everything can learn the reason for my song.

When I Die

There is a transparent tenderness in this poem from the very first line. Written by a man for the woman he loves, the veils of defense that can obscure a man's vulnerability have fallen away. If you are a man, and reading this poem, try reading it aloud to your beloved, in a way that speaks your own feelings for her. You will know the tenderness I refer to, as I knew it this morning while reading this sonnet of Neruda's to my wife in bed.

It is all the more poignant if, like me, you are years older than the one you love. If the natural order runs its course, then it is indeed likely that Maria will be closing my eyes for the last time with her "beloved hands." I shall never forget that within a few hours of our first meeting she said the strangest thing. She said she had a premonition that she would be with me when I died. I was shocked. I barely knew this woman, yet here she was implying, as it seemed to me, that she would know me for the rest of my life.

"Not necessarily," she said. "It may mean that I meet you again much later in life. Or that you call me when you know you are dying. I don't know what it means. I just tell you what I saw."

Now that we are married, her premonition seems more plausible. I have learned to trust the whisperings that seem to come to Maria's ear. It moves me, too, to know that she is courageous enough to love without reserve, while knowing in the same moment that she will probably survive me by many years.

Death, in any event, is always the shadow of love, however young or old we are; for everything, even that which we would wish to last forever, has its season, and no more. Or is it really so? Neruda's beautiful sonnet, in which love and death are entwined from beginning to end, takes up the time-honored romantic theme—that love survives all.

If someone is reading you this poem as lover to beloved, take in the words as a message from your lover's heart to yours, Neruda's sonnet being the bird that sings to you. Even if you are alone, you can say this poem out loud for yourself, and know that the beloved is ever present, whether visible now in your life or not. This is a gift to yourself of tenderness, rare in a world where our deeper sensibilities are blunted so easily by the clench of survival.

Pablo Neruda wrote this sonnet for the Chilean singer Matilde Urrutia. His *One Hundred Love Sonnets,* which includes this one, was published in 1960, when Neruda was in his fifties. Neruda had an international reputation as a political idealist, a diplomat, a man of letters and ideas, of big parties and global travel. He was in love with life, and he was always in love with a woman.

Neruda was accompanied by women throughout his life journey. He had an affair early in his life with the impossibly jealous and possessive Josie Bliss. Then he married a Dutch woman, Maria Antonieta Hagenaar, in 1930, who spoke no Spanish. When they separated in 1936, he lived with and then married the Argentinian painter, Delia del Carril, who was twenty years his senior. They separated in 1955, though for eight years prior to then he had continued a clandestine relationship with Matilde, to whom his *One Hundred Love Sonnets* is dedicated.

Matilde Urrutia was the inspiration for much of Neruda's later poetry. While he was still married to Delia, Neruda would send Matilde love poems daily. During this early part of their love affair, the great Mexican artist Diego Rivera painted Matilde's portrait with a profile of Neruda concealed in her thick dark hair. It was the lovers' secret. After their marriage, in 1966, Matilde remained his beloved companion until his death, in 1973. It was indeed she who held his hand as he passed out of this world.

When I die, I want your hands on my eyes:

These are blessing hands Neruda asks for. He is much older than Matilde, and he knows the time will come when his wife will hold him as he takes his last breath. The image of the hands on the eyes summons in my mind the gesture of the final closing of the beloved's eyes, the last kindness of one human being to another. And yet these hands offer more than the touch of kindness. Hands of light are healing hands.

They offer wheat and freshness, too. The mention of wheat is the only metaphor in the whole poem, and I wonder why Neruda, whose poetry normally ripples with metaphor, has offered only one in this poem. I imagine it carries an unusual significance. To me it summons the image of communion, increasing even further the sense of blessing. The hands nourish the loved one, too, as bread does; they send him on his way through the portal of death with soul food. I think of a boat being launched; of these hands sending the dying one on to a new life in which the soul sails free. Let your reading of this poem be leisurely, so that your own images can emerge in response to Neruda's.

I know what Neruda means when he speaks of "the softness that changed my destiny." When I looked up at the lunch table in a remote Michigan retreat center and met the woman who was to become my wife, I knew that nothing would be the same again. In that moment I came to know in a way I had never known before that I was loved. That, indeed, I had always been loved.

This sonnet is one of the most gloriously romantic poems ever written. Although Neruda was a self-proclaimed atheist and Marxist, he was also a poet, with a deep and far-reaching romantic sensibility. While the word *romantic* has lost its original vigor, and is often used now as a synonym for *saccharine,* the genuinely romantic is anything but sweet, and far from sentimental.

No great poet is sentimental, and least of all Neruda. Sentimentality does not have the ring of truth about it. It is too content to indulge in some abstract idea of love, rather than being willing to dive into the lived experience of it as it is, with all its tribulations as well as joys. Love, wrote James Merrill in one of his poems, is "a pearl whose cost / we doubt till it is bitten."[1] Neruda, of all people, did not hesitate to test his bite.

In the first half of the nineteenth century, Romanticism pervaded every aspect of European culture. At its heart lay a deep respect for authenticity, integrity, and the inner truth of love and faith, as distinct to the received truths of traditional art and religion. Whereas the eighteenth century placed the intellect above all other faculties, the passion of Romanticism was for mind-and-heart—what Wordsworth called "the feeling intellect."

"The feeling intellect" is the human soul, and this sonnet streams from the soul of Neruda. It was written thirteen years before his death, yet he can already savor the bittersweetness of his undying love.

I want you to live while I wait for you, asleep.

Neruda lived in two worlds: this one, and the world of the imagination, which is no less real. His love poetry, while indeed inspired by a flesh-and-blood woman, also carries the scent of the ideal; of that perfection which the imagination knows exists somewhere, but which never quite seems to incarnate fully in this world. For the Romantics, imagination was the chief of human faculties.

It is the imagination that allows us to see the world in a grain of sand, the imagination that crystallizes our feelings of wonder and admiration and projects them onto the beloved.

In loving this particular person, you also touch the eternal qualities that are both within the person and beyond them. This is the meeting of souls in a love that can prevail even over death. For the romantic, love of this kind is a genuine spiritual odyssey with its own ultimate promise of redemption and eternal life. For such a love can purify you, raise you up, make you whole, and live on in the other even after you are gone.

Neruda's sonnet flows this way, towards a triumph of love over death.

I want what I love to continue to live

Matilde was more than a flesh-and-blood woman for him. His vision of her—in this poem, at least, which is to say in the realm of imagination—endows her with the capacity to embody the eternal. Through her, and through his love for her, he and his song will live on.

These are universal themes that now, as ever, touch a chord in many hearts. Those who have not known such a love have probably felt the longing for it. Never mind the nineteenth century: the Romantic passion has been, if not the prevailing mood, then at least a powerful current in the Western world ever since. Romanticism speaks to something deep in the Western psyche: the longing for union, for self-knowledge, and for eternal life through love—love of another, of the world, of God, all in one. In America, the voices of Walt Whitman, Thoreau, and Emerson, whisper as ever on the wind. Today the Romantic influence still runs deep in the poetry of, among others, Mary Oliver, Galway Kinnell, Robert Bly, and Pablo Neruda.

That Neruda knows he will die does not mean he believes his love will end. No, he will continue to hear the wind, sniff the sea's aroma, walk on the sand with her, his beloved Matilde. Wherever she goes, he will be there, living through and with her every step of her way. Love will always outlive death. Love is the air of the soul, and the soul does not die because there is no end to love. Souls travel together through life after life sustained by love's breath. No one, in reality, goes anywhere when they die. "Where would they go?" the Indian saint Ramana Maharshi used to say.

What is found now is found then,[2]

said the poet Kabir. There is only love, and it is here and now. The presence of this moment gathers to itself the whole of the future as well as the past.

Every true lover wants his beloved to "flourish, full-flowered." For the lover who dies, however, the wish is more poignant. The beloved, in flourishing—in filling up with life—is able to pass on the love of the one who has died to everything she touches. She has that power because his love breathes in her. She can communicate merely by her presence—through her eyes, through her touch and her words, through everything she is and does—the reason for her beloved's song. Neruda will even travel as a shadow in Matilde's hair, just as he did in Diego Rivera's painting of her.

Pablo Neruda's sonnets are love songs. They serve no other purpose than to celebrate the truth, the beauty, the poignancy of love. In this more jaded time, you may wonder whether they belong more properly to some earlier, more "romantic" era. But the time of love is never over, and that is why Neruda's sonnets will continue to sing through the world as long as there are lovers who can hear his song.

9

THE THIRD BODY

by Robert Bly

A man and a woman sit near each other, and they
   do not long
At this moment to be older, or younger, or born
In any other nation, or any other time, or any other
   place.
They are content to be where they are, talking or
   not talking.
Their breaths together feed someone whom we do
   not know.
The man sees the way his fingers move;
He sees her hands close around a book she hands
   to him.
They obey a third body that they share in common.
They have promised to love that body.
Age may come; parting may come; death will come!
A man and a woman sit near each other;
As they breathe they feed someone we do not know,
Someone we know of, whom we have never seen.

This Presence

I have loved this poem for a dozen years and more. Like the touch of ice, it gives off an unusual heat, for all its apparent quiet and coolness. Remember Emily Dickinson, who said,

> If I read a book and it makes my whole body so cold no fire can warm me, I know that is poetry.[1]

The quality of heat in a poem matters. Robert Bly says as much in his introduction to *The Best of American Poetry 1999*. Poetry is a form of energy. At first glance this poem, "The Third Body," might not be what you would normally associate with a love poem; there seems to be no ardor, no passion, nothing happening. But in the stillness, the coolness of it, is the quiet intensity of a new moon.

The poem first appeared in the collection *Loving a Woman in Two Worlds,* published in 1987. A review in the *New York Times Book Review* said that it wasn't a real book of love poems because there wasn't enough hatred and anger in it. Bly's response in an interview of the time was revealing: "In a way he's right, but only in a thoroughly modern way. That book has links to the thirteenth-century French and German trou- badours. It's about seven centuries out of date."

The troubadours wrote verses in honor of flesh-and-blood women who at the same time carried for them the ideals of spiritual love. Their work was infused with an energy similar to that found in the ecstatic poetry of Rumi, who was living in the same era, though in what is now Turkey. It is no coinci- dence that, alongside the body of his own original work, Bly has devoted time and attention to making translations of Rumi.

Rumi—especially in translations by Bly and Coleman Barks—speaks of love in such a way that it forms an arc between the personal and the divine. Lovers can read his poetry to each other and know that Rumi is speaking to them. Lovers of the divine can read his work and know the same thing. Human and divine love, Rumi suggests, have the same origin, which is beyond all we can ever know.

"The Third Body," too, points to a source beyond all our knowing. Like the outpourings of the troubadours and the mystical poets, it fuses a personal love with a love that is beyond the physical form. The tone of this poem is tranquility, even silence. Yet there is no deeper, subtler energy that can move between two people than the presence that emerges from out of this quiet air.

The man and woman in this poem do not long for any- thing other than what they have. They do not long to be anything other than what they are. Being where they are in the simplicity and the fullness of the moment is entirely sufficient. Imagine the deep rest that is inherent in such a condition, how rare it is in this agitated world.

This couple is content, but not in a way that implies sleep or idleness. On the contrary, they are awake even to the movement of a finger. There is an attention in this quality of rest that resembles meditation; yet these two are not sitting cross-legged or kneeling in a posture of prayer. The scene is completely ordinary, two people sitting near each other, talking or not talking. Yet, whether they are speaking or not, the underlying rest and silence remain undisturbed. In India, they call this silence the soundless sound. In traditional music the world over, from the tamboura in India to the bagpipes in Scotland, it is represented by the drone instrument, the one that holds a single note.

Robert Bly was in his late forties when he wrote this poem. He had already won the National Book Award with a previous work, *The Light Around the Body,* and had achieved considerable notoriety with his antiwar poems and activism during the sixties. He had already lived a full life by the time this collection was published, and these love poems are the work of a maturing man. He had moved beyond the heat of youthful love to an intimacy (with Ruth, the woman who was to become his second wife) that could sense the breath of the spirit at its heart.

> *Their breaths together feed someone whom we do*
> *not know.*

Bly's spirituality is uniquely his own, with influences from the Sufis, the Gnostics, Jacob Boehme, the Christian mystic, and also Carl Jung. A personal sense of the divine runs through his work. For Bly, the world is full of presences, seen and unseen. But who is this "someone" in "The Third Body" that the breath of love goes to feed? We do not know, Bly says.

The line fills this couple's room with an invisible and nameless energy, and we sense that everything, even the most ordinary moment, can serve to nourish worlds that exist alongside and within our own, even if we ourselves may have no knowledge of them. Is this someone "the third body" of the title? The spirit of their relationship, which encompasses both of them? At this stage of the poem, Bly is insisting we don't know.

> *The man sees the way his fingers move;*
> *He sees her hand close around a book she hands to him.*

The man is an observer to the movement of his own fingers. He does not move them; they move. You may know this quiet, in which life seems to live itself, and you can rest in the simplicity of watching it unfold. The whole body is nourished by such moments, and in this simplicity, an attention can emerge in which you are awake to everything, however insignificant it may appear to be. Anything within the field of this presence— even the gesture of a hand closing around a book—can assume a substance beyond its normal means. Perhaps you have known this for yourself—a moment, an hour, when the air you shared with your lover was charged with silence and every gesture seemed effortless, even weightless.

This is the flavor of the third body that these two lovers share. The third brings to mind the Holy Spirit, the unifying force that is beyond all notions of right and wrong, good and bad. Its symbol is the white dove of peace, the peace that passes understanding. The mind, which is bound by the laws of duality, can never grasp the domain that transcends the opposites. That domain is a third force, and its signature is a feeling of spaciousness, for it can include everything. As this man and woman have room for talking or not talking.

In naming the third body, Bly is speaking to the spiritual and the personal at the same time. When two people love each other in this way, they discover a unity that is more than a mere merging. Their individuality may even intensify in such a love, yet at the same time they meet beyond themselves, in this third place. Just as the Christian Trinity is a unity that emerges not in spite of, but because of the duality. This kind of love is a deep stream. It can hold everything that flows along its course, without judgment; the difficult and the testing as well as the good and the beautiful. What a grace, for a couple to know this.

> *They obey a third body that they share in common.*
> *They have promised to love that body.*
> *Age may come; parting may come; death will come!*

The lines echo something of the Christian marriage vows, yet no mention of marriage is made here. The nature of this love is itself a sacrament. Its binding force does not come from any external pressure, societal or otherwise. Rather, the couple's promise "to love that body" is a natural response to its spacious, invisible beauty. When this third body emerges between two people, they want to honor its presence in their life by nourishing it, sustaining it with their attention and love. They want to listen for its quiet voice, the one that can be heard in the deep heart. "Listening," after all, is the original, root meaning of *obedience.*

Bly tells us for a second time that this man and woman are sitting near each other, as if to impress upon us that they are not in physical contact. They do not need to be. They are touching each other, feeling each other, through the third body that exists between them. This love does not deny physical love, but it does not need it, either. Perhaps their shared presence will lead to making love. Or perhaps it won't. There is neither any desire nor any fear of desire throughout the poem. This couple breathes a subtler air.

I love the way Bly ends "The Third Body" with a mystery and a paradox. He repeats the substance of an earlier line, saying that we do not know the one whom their breaths go to feed. And yet, he now adds, we know of the being, even though we have never seen it. Surely he is speaking of the third body here. Would we, the reader and the poet, necessarily know of this third body? I think so. Even if we have not experienced such a love in our lives, I suspect we know of it.

That knowledge is built into the fabric of our humanness, so we can feel the tremor of it in a poem even if it has not yet touched our life in manifest form. This is why so many of us live with a longing for the love that encompasses both worlds. You can long for something, after all, only if you know in your bones it already exists.

10

BUOYANCY

by Rumi *(Version by Coleman Barks)*

Love has taken away all my practices
And filled me with poetry.

I tried to keep quietly repeating,
No strength but yours,
But I couldn't.

I had to clap and sing.
I used to be respectable and chaste and stable,
but who can stand in this strong wind
and remember those things?

A mountain keeps an echo deep inside itself.
That's how I hold your voice.

I am scrap wood thrown in your fire,
and quickly reduced to smoke.

I saw you and became empty.
This emptiness, more beautiful than existence,
it obliterates existence, and yet when it comes,
existence thrives and creates more existence.

The sky is blue. The world is a blind man
squatting on the road.

But whoever sees your emptiness
sees beyond blue and beyond the blind man.

A great soul hides like Mohammed, or Jesus,
moving through a crowd in a city
where no one knows him.

To praise is to praise
how one surrenders
to the emptiness.

To praise the sun is to praise your own eyes.
Praise, the ocean. What we say, a little ship.

So the sea-journey goes on, and who knows where!
Just to be held by the ocean is the best luck
we could have. It's a total waking up!

Why should we grieve that we've been sleeping?
It doesn't matter how long we've been unconscious.

We're groggy, but let the guilt go.
Feel the motions of tenderness
around you, the buoyancy.

Love Has Taken Away
All My Practices

There are many "practices" to bolster love. The shelves of
bookstores are groaning with self-help strategies, five-point
plans to improve our relationship or to make ourselves more
attractive to the opposite sex. But love is more like an electri-
cal storm than a pension plan. It has scant regard for our
rational intentions. When it comes, almost always unbidden,
love will upset our comfortable routines. Like so much con-
fetti, it will fling into the air all our fantasies of what our life
is meant to look like.

What is true of human love is also true of the love divine.
While most of the other poems in this book primarily
address human love, Rumi's words spring from—and sum-
mon us toward—divine love. The "practices" he speaks of
here are spiritual disciplines. Every tradition has its own bat-
tery of techniques with which to dismantle the ego's preoc-
cupation with itself. In one, you count your breaths or repeat
the name of God, in another you attend church on Sunday
or press the length of your body to the earth five times a day.

And every tradition has its own way of shaping the relationship between personal effort and divine grace. One

school of thought will tell you that revelation, enlighten-
ment, union with God, come about gradually, through the
discipline of its practices. Another will say that everything is
due to the workings of grace, and that it either happens
instantly or not at all.

We won't join that debate here, except to point out that
Rumi was a master of spiritual practices until love took them
all away from him. In matters of the deep heart, life rarely
conforms to ready-made answers. There is a Sufi saying that
captures the whole paradox:

> If you seek Him you shall never find Him. But if
> you do not seek Him, He will never reveal himself
> to you.

Rumi's poem, like this saying, echoes deep in me. When I
read it aloud to myself, and slowly, I sense tremors of meaning
that bypass my mind on their way straight to my marrow. Then
there are the chords I recognize from the life that I have lived,
and these I can shape into consonant and vowel. In sifting
your own meanings from Rumi's words, you are likely to hear
other melodies than the ones that reached my ears.

This is good, and as it should be. Your differences with my
interpretations, as much as any nod of recognition, will help
shape, even provoke, your own variations on the poet's
themes. Your own unique life will always draw out harmonies
I can never know. This is the art and alchemy of poetry:
through the spaces between the words, borne along on a
wave of rhythm and sound, the life breath of the reader joins

that of the poet. In this union of forces, an awakening can happen that is not only new from reader to reader, but in a great poem, from reading to reading.

> *Love has taken away all my practices*
> *And filled me with poetry.*

Love has blown all the words out of my mouth more than once. Love has left me dumbfounded, with eyes like full moons. In those moments, or hours—even weeks—I was returned to a naked simplicity, all preoccupations falling away. It is from this naked state, I believe, that great poetry is born. This is the spring from which Rumi's ecstatic words burst into the world.

Rumi had lived a life of serious study and ascetic practices before he ever met Shams of Tabriz, the man who was to set his heart on fire. Rumi had followed in his father's footsteps, and was the head of a center of religious learning in the city of Konya, Turkey. One version of his first meeting with Shams is that Rumi was giving a lecture to his students by a fountain in the city. Shams appeared, walked up to the revered teacher, and threw his books into the water, saying it was time for Rumi to start living what he had been reading about for so long.

The moment his eyes met those of Shams, Rumi's life changed forever. The veils fell away and he stood naked in the fire of love. All his poetry stems from that source. Before then, he had written only scholarly treatises. In the words of another ecstatic Sufi saint, the poet Hafiz, Shams had "lit the lamp that needs no oil."[1] Once ignited, love of this kind needs no external source of fuel; it is self-generating, eternal, requiring no object or any exercise of the human will.

In this sense, love is always a miracle. It is always above and beyond the natural state, beyond all our notions of right and wrong. Rumi was an exemplary teacher before he met Shams, a truly good man. But he had not known love. Love shook him to his very foundations. It made him a madman in the eyes of some of his followers. Instead of giving eloquent lectures, Rumi would spin around a column in the mosque singing out his love-praises in verse. Out of jealousy, his students murdered Shams. It was then that Rumi's best poetry poured from his broken heart, a heart that joined him to the suffering and beauty of this world and the next.

I feel a special affinity with the first few lines of this poem—in part, I acknowledge, because they can be taken to justify my own lack of discipline and hesitant spiritual fire. I have never been moved to sustain a particular spiritual tradition or practice.

> *I tried to keep quietly repeating,*
> No strength but yours,
> *But I couldn't.*

I have been a fool in this matter of spiritual love, just as I have in the human sphere. Often not knowing which way to turn or how to proceed. I have never had the discipline or even an inclination to harness the inner wish to any one tradition or regular "practice."

I wanted to murmur the Jesus prayer under my breath, "Lord have mercy upon me." But the words would slip away. At another time in my life, I started with a Hindu mantra; another year, it was watching my breath. Every time, underneath any effort I made, a voice would whisper, "Not that, not that. No turn of your mind, no seeking will find me." Yet who was this "me"? Always, still now, there is no name or image that comes to my mind. Only this persistent, unbidden prompting, sometimes vibrant, often barely discernable, that rubs away at me through my days and that, when I follow it, leads only to silence. Not to answers, mind you, but rather, on a good day, to a wordless question, an interior readiness for . . . for what?

My inner life is still in some ways the rag and bone shop it always was. In the afternoon of my life, I am already undone. I will never know for myself the kind of dedication that Rumi gave to his spiritual disciplines before meeting Shams; nor have I known that fiery glance of a master that burned Rumi to nothing. Perhaps I can have no inkling of Rumi's true meaning. I take solace, even so, in these first lines of Rumi, using them as I do to fit my own purposes and shortcomings.

I used to be respectable and chaste and stable,

I still am, in large part. How about you? Oh, I have been stirred by fiery poetry, the fierce gaze of teachers, the rapture of the occasional realization. Yet my survival instincts remain intact. They have even been known to marshal spiritual states to the defense of my identity as a solid individual. An individual who has "had experiences." Then, how warming, how nourishing, it is, to have the respect of others. To convey an aura of authority, to have a place in the world.

None of this can withstand the breath of love, Rumi says. And he should know, for he had honors in large measure before Shams came along. How willing are we to let the whole world go for love? I don't think we can know the answer to that before it happens. Lord have mercy! Is there no way out from under our own plots and schemings?

There is, there is, Rumi says. There is a way: fall backward into love. That strong wind blows where it wills, and if you pray for it to come your way, beware: if your prayer is answered, it will leave no trace of you behind.

> *I am scrap wood thrown in your fire,*
> *and quickly reduced to smoke.*

I have not died the death Rumi died when his eyes met the gaze of Shams. I am still sitting here writing these words in well-formed sentences. Yet I suspect that both you and I know, somewhere in our depths, of this all-consuming fire. Our longing for love is already the curl of its smoke on the wind. All true love is a dying—to self-preoccupation, to the known and predictable, to the picture we have had of ourselves thus far. Rumi's poetry erupts, volcanolike, from these fiery depths.

> *I saw you and became empty.*
> *This emptiness, more beautiful than existence,*

it obliterates existence, and yet when it comes,
existence thrives and creates more existence.

When Rumi says " I saw you," he means Shams, but not just Shams, the person. He means the fire that shone through Shams's eyes, the glance that pierced him to the core. Though its spark can leap from person to person, that fire is spiritual in origin, and not personal. Could it have been anybody, then, who received love's fire from Shams? In the realm of potential, maybe. In actuality, in that time and place, Rumi was the one person ripe for burning.

Shams had been told in a vision that he would find his only true spiritual friend—someone who would recognize the love that had already burned him away—in the city of Konya. The vision also told him he would need to be ready to die for that grace. Shams, the psychological entity, had already died in that fire, so physical death held no fear for him. He immediately set out for Konya, and knew who Rumi was as soon as he saw him.

Rumi became empty when he looked into Shams's eyes. The Sufi word for this emptiness is *fana*. It is the state of no difference, when there is no one looking out onto the world because seer and seen have dissolved into one. Then you are bound to love your neighbor as yourself, not as an exercise, but because your neighbor *is* you.

I had a glimpse of this emptiness once in the vastness of the Sahara. I had been walking for an hour or more across a flat, empty plain that stretched as far behind and in front of me as my eyes could see. My thoughts had ebbed away in the silence, and all that was left was the walking, and even that was aimless, for there was nowhere to go. The walking, and the desert. Then suddenly I noticed a slight rise on the horizon, and in the same moment my sense of self returned. Even the contour of a hill can be enough of a reference point— enough of an other—to bring us back into sharp relief again.

Not from the emptiness that Rumi knew, however. I would like to think that his emptiness was not a passing state, but a permanent, absolute condition. Rumi, the reputable scholar, died forever in that moment of truth when he fell into the pool of his master's eyes. The Beloved became everything for him, and even the lover died.

Rumi seems to speak in riddles here. On the one hand, he says this emptiness "obliterates existence"; on the other, he says that it creates even more existence. You will bring your own understanding to bear on this paradox. The lines remind me of a conversation I had many years ago in London with Irina Tweedie, the Sufi mystic. We were speaking about *fana,* the emptiness. I wondered whether this state would bring about a lack of enthusiasm or interest for the world.

"Oh, no," she replied. " I understand that it might seem that way but in practice it is just the opposite. Life is never so real or beautiful. The difference, however, is that we are no longer chasing after it and its pleasures. We have the taste of something infinitely more precious. My life is at its end, but I tell you that flowers have never looked so red; nor has food ever tasted as good as it does now. And yet, I am not chasing these things, the things of the world. There is something I cannot name which is lovelier still. It is nowhere else; it is here, but it is not of this world."[2]

I think this is what Rumi means when he speaks of seeing beyond the blue sky and the blind man. In that condition of emptiness (being empty of self) our eyes are not restricted to the world of form. We can see through and beyond appearances; we realize the unifying wisdom that encompasses everything that is and ever shall be. Yet the form world is not excluded from that beatific vision. It is gathered up in it, so that the world is even more beautiful somehow for the light that shines through it. In this way of seeing, what ordinarily appear to be different realms, material and spiritual, are now understood to be one and the same. No difference, either, in that moment, between human and spiritual love.

To surrender to that emptiness is in itself an act of praise. Yet how do we sing those kinds of praises? We don't. This is the kind of praising that "sings us"—we fall backward without forethought, arms and mouth wide open. When that moment comes, there is nothing else to do but to become the song that has been wanting to sing us our whole life long.

So the sea-journey goes on, and who knows where!

You can never know where the love journey will take you. All you can know is that you are sailing in uncharted waters and that you are still breathing! Love holds you up! But you can't know that till you dive into its waters. Its depths are as clear and crisp as you will ever know. Love is "a total waking up!"

How kind, how forgiving, these last few lines are. There can be no love without kindness, as Naomi Shihab Nye has conveyed so movingly in her poem earlier in this book. And you are the first one in line for your own kindness and forgiveness. If you are like me, you may wonder at times whether you have missed the true love boat altogether, however many earthly loves you may or may not have known.

Why should we grieve that we've been sleeping?
It doesn't matter how long we've been unconscious.

"Let the guilt go!" cries Rumi. There is always time to come aboard, whoever you are, no matter how lonely. Even in this moment, "let your arms rest, and your heart, and heart's little intelligence," as Mary Oliver puts it in our first poem; be at peace and

Feel the motions of tenderness
around you, the buoyancy.

This is such a compassionate view of life, and I believe it is true. It says we are already held, whether we know it or not, however unconscious or awake we are. If we can just look up for a moment, we may feel how everything sustains us, keeps us afloat, even in our darkest hours. The air passes in and out of us, ever patient; the world keeps turning, the sun rises.

If we ever give ourselves to the tenderness of these waters completely, then even whether we live or die won't matter anymore. This is the love beyond mortal love that united

Rumi and Shams. The Sufi poet Hafiz knew this love too. Let him have the last word:

> *We have turned our face to the pearl lying on the*
> *ocean floor.*
> *So why then should we worry if this wobbly old boat*
> *keeps going or not?*[3]

May you and I each catch sight one day, or now, of that priceless beauty.

Epilogue

It is not easy to keep your heart open in the face of the trials of being human. Life can so often be difficult, disappointing; our dreams are so easily broken. How precious, then, those shafts of sunlight that sometimes break through our daily preoccupations, our anxieties, and reveal the beauty that was there all along.

Neither beauty nor love—for the eyes that see beauty are the eyes of love—need the absence of pain or suffering to exist. This, I believe, is the enduring message of the poets in this book. Sometimes we know the grace of sheer joy; sometimes, we are so in love with our lover, with life, with God, that we want to leap into the air and tell the whole world. When the phone call comes that seems to break our world apart, or when we feel such an absence of the living presence that life no longer seems worth living, does it mean that the love we once knew has gone away?

No, say the poets, this is not what it means. Even in the midst of our suffering, love can bloom. Our weeping, as well as our laughing, can open our heart to a deeper stream.

When we finally stop struggling with life, stop wanting it to be anything but what it is now—not giving up but giving it over—then our heart will indeed fall open, and we shall know beyond all doubt that, however dark the night, all is already well.

Let us end with Rumi, and with these lines from his poem "Zero Circle":

> *Be helpless, dumbfounded, unable to say yes or no.*
> *Then a stretcher will come from grace and gather us up.*

That will be the moment when we can let the guilt go and "feel the motions of tenderness" that have been around us all along.

About the Poets

MARY OLIVER (b. 1935)
"West Wind #2"

Mary Oliver is one of America's most widely read contemporary poets. The poet and critic Alicia Ostriker has called her "as visionary as Emerson." She won her first poetry prize at the age of twenty-seven, from the Poetry Society of America, for her collection *No Voyage and Other Poems*. She won the Pulitzer prize in 1984 for her collection of poems *American Primitive*, and she was winner of the 1992 National Book Award for Poetry for her *New and Selected Poems*. Her more recent works include *The Leaf and the Cloud* and *What Do We Know*. She is a professor at Bennington College in Vermont.

SHARON OLDS (b. 1942)
"The Knowing"

Sharon Olds was the New York State poet laureate from 1998 to 2000. She is the author of seven volumes of poetry, the second of which, *The Dead and the Living* (1984), won the Lamont Poetry Prize and the National Book Critics Circle Award. She currently holds the Chair of New York University's Creative Writing Program. The poet and novelist Michael Ondaatje has said that "Sharon Olds' poems are pure fire in the hands—risky, on the verge of failing, and in the end leaping up. I love the roughness and humor and brag and tenderness and completion in her work as she carries the reader through rooms of passion and loss."

GALWAY KINNELL (b. 1927)

"Saint Francis and the Sow"

Galway Kinnell received the Pulitzer prize in 1983 for his *Selected Poems*. He has been poet in residence at several universities, as well as a field-worker for the Congress of Racial Equality. Robert Langbaum said in the *American Poetry Review*, "Kinnell, at a time when so many poets are content to be skillful and trivial, speaks with a big voice about the whole of life." Throughout his work, he explores his relationship to transience, to death, to the power of wilderness and wildness, and to the primitive underpinnings of existence. He once said that "if you could keep going deeper, you would finally not be a person . . . you'd be a blade of grass or ultimately, perhaps, a stone. And if a stone could read, poetry would speak for it."

WISLAWA SZYMBORSKA (b. 1923)

"Love at First Sight"

Wislawa Szymborska has lived in the city of Krakow, in southern Poland, since 1931. From 1953 to 1981 she was poetry editor for the Krakow literary weekly *Zycie Literackie*. She has written sixteen collections of poetry and has received many honors, including the Goethe Prize in 1991, the Polish PEN Club Prize in 1996, and the Nobel Prize for Literature, also in 1996. Always keen to avoid publicity, she left for a country retreat when news of her Nobel honor reached the media. She has disclaimed her debut work in 1952, and its successor in 1954, as attempts to conform to social realism at a time when Communist censorship held sway in Poland. Though for many years she used a deceptively casual tone to convey her skepticism concerning mankind, her later work is more personal and conveys her belief in the power of words and in the joys arising from the imagination. She has been married twice, and has been a widow since the early nineties. Her most recent works are *Miracle Fair: Selected Poems of Wislawa Szymborska* and *Poems New and Collected, 1957–1997*.

CZESLAW MILOSZ (b. 1911)
"Love"

Milosz's first work was published in 1933 in Poland, where his family moved soon after his birth. In 1951, after joining the diplomatic service of People's Poland in 1945, he sought asylum in France, where he wrote several works of prose. In 1953, he received the Prix Littéraire Européen. In 1960, he moved to Berkeley, California, where he became Professor of Slavic Languages and Literature at the University of California. He has won many awards and prizes, culminating in the Nobel Prize for Literature in 1980. His most recent poetry collection is the *New and Collected Poems 1931–2001*, while his new prose work is *To Begin Where I Am: Selected Essays*. He writes poetry, Milosz says in *The Collected Poems 1931–87* (Ecco Press, 1988), "to find my home in one sentence, concise, as if hammered in metal. Not to enchant anybody. Not to earn a lasting name in posterity. An unnamed need for order, for rhythm, for form, which three words are opposed to chaos and nothingness."

NAOMI SHIHAB NYE (b. 1952)
"Kindness"

Nye was born of a Palestinian father and an American mother. Her work consistently reveals the poignancy and the paradoxes that emerge from feeling an intimate relationship with two different cultures. She was born in St. Louis, has lived in Jerusalem, and lives with her family now in San Antonio. All three places weave in and out of her writing. Her poems and short stories have appeared in reviews and magazines all over the world. Besides her six volumes of poetry, she has also written books for children and edited several anthologies of prose. Nye thinks of her poetry as political because "politics is about people, and I am interested in the personal ramifications of everything, for everybody." She first started writing poetry at the age of six. "Somehow I knew what a poem was. I liked the comfortable, portable shape of poems. I liked the space around them and the way you could hold your words at arm's length and look at them. And especially the way they took you to a deeper, quieter place, almost immediately."

DENISE LEVERTOV (1923–1997)
"The Ache of Marriage"

Denise Levertov, born in Wales, was educated entirely at home by her mother, a sophisticated woman of letters, and her father, a Jew who converted to Christianity to become an Anglican minister. She wrote her first book, *The Double Image,* between the ages of seventeen and twenty-one. It was published in 1946. After emigrating to America, and becoming a naturalized citizen in 1956, she was soon recognized as an important voice in the American avant-garde. Her next book, *With Eyes in the Back of Our Heads,* established her as one of the great American poets, and her British origins were forgotten. In the sixties and seventies, activism and feminism became prominent in her work. She published more than twenty volumes of poetry, and from 1989 to 1993, she taught at Stanford University. She spent the last decade of her life in Seattle, Washington. She was always an outsider, in England, in America, and also in poetry circles, for she never considered herself part of any school. She said, "These feelings of not-belonging were positive for me, not negative. . . . I was given such a sense of confidence by my family, in my family, that though I was often shy . . . I nevertheless experienced the sense of difference as an honor, as part of knowing at an early age—perhaps by seven, certainly before I was ten—that I was an artist-person and had a destiny."

PABLO NERUDA (1904–1973)
"Love Sonnet LXXXIX"

Pablo Neruda is widely considered the most important Latin American poet of the twentieth century, as well as an influential contributor to major developments in modern poetry. He was born in the provincial town of Parral, Chile, the son of a teacher and a railway worker. He moved to the capital, Santiago, for his university education and published his first poetry collection, *Crepusculario,* in 1923 at the age of nineteen. *Twenty Love Poems and a Song of Despair,* which has since been translated into dozens of languages, came out the following year. Between 1927 and 1935 he held a series of honorary consulships around the world, and in 1943 he returned

to Chile, soon to become a senator of the Republic and a member of
the Communist Party of Chile. His political interests strongly colored the
poetic output of his middle years, though his complete oeuvre, running to
several thousand pages, spans a vast range of ideas and passions.

ROBERT BLY (b. 1926)
"The Third Body"

Robert Bly, poet, editor, translator, storyteller, father of what he has called
the "expressive men's movement," was born in western Minnesota to parents of Norwegian stock. At Harvard, he joined a famous group of under-
graduate writers—Donald Hall, Kenneth Koch, Adrienne Rich, John
Ashbery, and others. In 1956 he went on a Fulbright scholarship to Norway
to translate Norwegian poetry into English. There he found the work of
many poets, including Neruda, César Vallejo, and Georg Trakl, who were
unknown in the United States. He returned to start a literary review, *The
50's*, then *The 60's*, and *The 70's*, which introduced the works of these poets
to his generation. Bly has always believed that a poet should follow Rilke's
advice, "to go into yourself." Neruda, Lorca, and Antonio Machado were
examples of this more interior way. In 1966, Bly cofounded the American
Writers Against the Vietnam War, and led much of the opposition among
writers to it. During the seventies he had eleven books of poetry, essays, and
translations published. During the eighties four more collections were published. His most recent collection, of new and selected poems, is *Eating the
Honey of Words*. His latest translations, of Ghalib, are in *The Lightning Should
Have Fallen on Ghalib*.

RUMI (1207–1273)

"Buoyancy"

Rumi was the founder of the Sufi Order known as the Mevlevi (Whirling Dervishes) in Konya, Turkey, in the thirteenth century. Though the theme of lover and beloved was already an established one in Sufi teaching, his own poetry was inspired by his meeting with and the consequent loss of his great teacher, Shams of Tabriz. Out of their relationship was born some of the most inspired love poetry ever, in which Rumi sings of a love that is both personal and divine at the same time. After Shams's death, he would burst into ecstatic poetry anywhere, any time—and his scribe and disciple, Husam, was charged with writing it all down. Rumi's great spiritual treatise, *The Mathnawi,* written in couplets, amounts to more than twenty-five thousand lines in six books.

Notes

INTRODUCTION

1. Excerpt from the poem "Awake Awhile." In *I Heard God Laughing: Renderings of Hafiz*. Daniel Ladinsky. Oakland, Calif.: Dharma Printing Co., 1996.
2. Excerpt from *The Leaf and the Cloud*. Mary Oliver. New York: Da Capo Press, 2000.
3. Excerpt from the poem "Love Dogs." Rumi. In *The Essential Rumi*. Trans. Coleman Barks. San Francisco: HarperSanFrancisco, 1995.
4. Excerpt from "Desire and the Importance of Failing." Rumi. In *Feeling the Shoulder of the Lion*. Trans. Coleman Barks. Boston: Threshold/Shambhala Publications, 1991.

1 "WEST WIND #2"

1. Excerpt from *A Poetry Handbook*. Mary Oliver. New York: Harvest Books, 1995.
2. Excerpt from the poem "Wild Geese." In *New and Selected Poems*. Mary Oliver. Boston: Beacon Press, 1992.

2 "THE KNOWING"

1. *Joseph Campbell and the Power of Myth* Tape 5: "Love and the Goddess." New York: Mystic Fire Audio, 1988.
2. Excerpt from *The Leaf and the Cloud*. Mary Oliver. New York: Da Capo Press, 2000.

3 "SAINT FRANCIS AND THE SOW"

1. Excerpt from *Leaves of Grass*. 1892 ed. Walt Whitman. New York: Modern Library.
2. Excerpt from the poem "The Métier of Blossoming." Denise Levertov. In *This Great Unknowing: Last Poems*. New York: New Directions, 1998.

5 "LOVE"

1. Excerpt from *On Love and Other Difficulties*. Rainer Maria Rilke. Trans. John J. L. Mood. New York: Norton & Co., 1975.
2. Excerpt from the poem "Wild Geese." In *New and Selected Poems*. Mary Oliver. Boston: Beacon Press, 1992.

6 "KINDNESS"

1. Excerpt from the poem "On the Beach." In *The Lives of the Heart*. Jane Hirshfield. New York: HarperPerennial, 1997.
2. Excerpt from the poem "The Same Inside." Anna Swir. In *Talking to My Body*. Trans. Czeslaw Milosz and Leonard Nathan. Port Townsend, Wash.: Copper Canyon Press, 1996.
3. *Hannah's Gift*. Maria Housden. New York: Bantam Dell, 2002.

7 "THE ACHE OF MARRIAGE"

1. Excerpt from the poem "About Marriage." In *Poems 1960–67*. Denise Levertov. New York: New Directions, 1983.
2. Excerpt from "A Poet's View." In *New and Selected Essays*. Denise Levertov. New York: New Directions, 1984.
3. Excerpt from *Letters to a Young Poet*. Rainer Maria Rilke. Trans. Stephen Mitchell. New York: Vintage Books, 1997.
4. Excerpt from Rainer Maria Rilke letter. In *Into the Garden: A Wedding Anthology*. Eds. Robert Hass and Stephen Mitchell. New York: HarperCollins, 1993.
5. Excerpt from the poem "Wanting All." In *Claiming the Spirit Within*. Ed. Marilyn Sewell. Boston: Beacon Press, 1996.
6. Excerpt from the poem "Listening to the Köln Concert." In *Eating the Honey of Words: New and Selected Poems*. Robert Bly. New York: HarperCollins, 1999.

7. Excerpt from Rilke letter. In *Into the Garden*. Eds. Robert Hass and Stephen Mitchell.

8. Excerpt from *The Prophet*. Kahlil Gibran. New York: Alfred A. Knopf, 1923.

9. Excerpt from Rilke letter. In *Into the Garden*. Eds. Robert Hass and Stephen Mitchell.

10. Excerpt from the poem "Last Night as I Was Sleeping." Antonio Machado. In *Times Alone: Selected Poems of Antonio Machado*. Trans. Robert Bly. Middletown, Conn.: Wesleyan University Press, 1983.

8 "LOVE SONNET LXXXIX"

1. Excerpt from the poem "Suspense of Love." James Merrill. In *Collected Poems*. New York: Alfred A. Knopf, 2001.

2. Excerpt from the poem "The Time Before Death." Kabir. From *The Kabir Book*. Trans. Robert Bly. Boston: Beacon Press, 1977.

9 "THE THIRD BODY"

1. Excerpt from *How to Read a Poem*. Edward Hirsch. New York: Double-Take Books, 1999, p. 7.

10 "BUOYANCY"

1. Excerpt from the poem "The Lamp That Needs No Oil." Hafiz. In *The Gift: Poems by Hafiz the Great Sufi Master*. Trans. Daniel Ladinsky. New York: Penguin Books, 1999.

2. Excerpt from *Fire in the Heart: Everyday Life as Spiritual Practice*. Roger Housden. Shaftesbury, U.K.: Element Books, 1990.

3. Excerpt from the poem "The Pearl on the Ocean Floor." Hafiz. In *The Soul Is Here for Its Own Joy: Sacred Poems from Many Cultures*. Ed. Robert Bly. New York: Ecco Press, 1995.

Recommended Reading

MARY OLIVER
The Leaf and the Cloud
New and Selected Poems
A Poetry Handbook
West Wind: Poems and Prose Poems
What Do We Know

SHARON OLDS
Blood, Tin, Straw
The Father
The Gold Cell
The Wellspring

GALWAY KINNELL
Mortal Acts, Mortal Words
A New Selected Poems
When One Has Lived a Long Time

WISLAWA SZYMBORSKA
Miracle Fair: Selected Poems of Wislawa Szymborska. Trans. Joanna Trzeciak.
Poems New and Collected: 1957–1997. Trans. Stanislaw Barańczak and
   Clare Cavanagh.
View with a Grain of Sand: Selected Poems. Trans. Stanislaw Barańczak and
   Clare Cavanagh.

CZESLAW MILOSZ
Milosz's ABC's
New and Collected Poems 1931–2001
Striving Toward Being: The Letters of Thomas Merton and Czeslaw Milosz

NAOMI SHIHAB NYE
Fuel
Words Under the Words: Selected Poems

DENISE LEVERTOV
O Taste and See
Poems: 1972–1982
The Stream and the Sapphire: Selected Poems on Religious Themes
This Great Unknowing: Last Poems

PABLO NERUDA
Full Woman, Fleshly Apple, Hot Moon: Selected Poems of Pablo Neruda.
    Trans. Stephen Mitchell.
Love: 10 Poems
100 Love Sonnets. Trans. Stephen Tapscott.
Twenty Love Poems and a Song of Despair. Trans. W. S. Merwin.

ROBERT BLY
Eating the Honey of Words
The Light Around the Body
Loving a Woman in Two Worlds
Morning Poems

RUMI
The Essential Rumi. Trans. Coleman Barks.
Like This. Trans. Coleman Barks.
Love's Glory: Re-Creations of Rumi. Trans. Andrew Harvey.
The Soul of Rumi. Trans. Coleman Barks.

Other Poets to Open Your Heart: A Brief List

GHALIB
The Lightning Should Have Fallen on Ghalib: Selected Poems of Ghalib.
Trans. Robert Bly.

HAFIZ
The Gift: Poems by Hafiz the Great Sufi Master. Trans. Daniel Ladinsky.
The Subject Tonight Is Love: 60 Wild and Sweet Poems of Hafiz.
Trans. Daniel Ladinsky.

SEAMUS HEANEY
The Spirit Level

JANE HIRSHFIELD
Given Sugar, Given Salt
The Lives of the Heart
The October Palace

KABIR
The Kabir Book: Forty-four of the Ecstatic Poems of Kabir. Trans. Robert Bly.

ANTONIO MACHADO
Antonio Machado: Selected Poems. Trans. Alan S. Trueblood.
Times Alone: Selected Poems of Antonio Machado. Trans. Robert Bly.

RAINER MARIA RILKE

Letters to a Young Poet. Trans. Stephen Mitchell.
On Love and Other Difficulties. Trans. John J. L. Mood.
Rilke's Book of Hours: Love Poems to God. Trans. Anita Barrows and
  Joanna R. Macy.
The Selected Poetry of Rainer Maria Rilke. Trans. Stephen Mitchell.

ANTHOLOGIES

Bly, Robert. *The Soul Is Here for Its Own Joy: Sacred Poems from Many Cultures*
Bly, Robert. *News of the Universe: Poems of Twofold Consciousness*
Hass, Robert, and Stephen Mitchell. *Into the Garden: A Wedding Anthology*
Hirshfield, Jane. *Women in Praise of the Sacred: 43 Centuries of Spiritual Poetry
  by Women*
Maltz, Wendy. *Passionate Hearts: The Poetry of Sexual Love*
Milosz, Czeslaw. *A Book of Luminous Things*
Mitchell, Stephen. *The Enlightened Heart: An Anthology of Sacred Poetry*

RECOMMENDED POETRY WORKSHOPS

By Heart: Poetry as Prayer, Passion and Spiritual Practice
Classes, workshops, and retreats offered by Kim Rosen (see acknowledg-
ments, page 141). Kim is a poet, teacher, and group facilitator who speaks
poetry by heart in gatherings throughout the world. Her workshops are an
opportunity to discover poetry as a powerful force for personal and spiritual unfolding through intimate exploration of the music, meaning,
breath, and voice inside the poems we love and the poems we write. For
information contact Delphirose@pocketmail.com.

Acknowledgments

I am indebted first and foremost to the ten poets whose work I include in this book. Kim Rosen and Lee Macey, your far-ranging editorial comments contributed enormously to the final work and have reminded me constantly that writing is, as Robert Bly once said, greatly enhanced through being in community. Toinette Lippe, I could not have wished for a more committed and grounded editor than you. Kim Witherspoon, my agent, I am grateful for your staunch support of the project from start to finish. Finally, I could never have embarked on a book such as this without the joy and sadness I have known with the women I have loved and been loved by. And without you, Maria, my wife and beloved companion, any such book from my hands would certainly have been much the poorer.

Permissions

About the Author

Roger Housden, a native of Bath, England, emigrated to the United States in 1998. He now lives in Woodstock, New York, with his wife, Maria. He is the author of several works of non-fiction, including *Ten Poems to Change Your Life*, and also a recent novella, *Chasing Rumi: A Fable About Finding the Heart's True Desire*. He gives occasional public recitals of ecstatic poetry from the world's great literary and spiritual traditions. You can e-mail him at tenpoems@juno.com.